SAND in my SHOE

D1603442

"A double garage with a family of five and grocery store." Business district of Twentynine Palms, December 1927.

SAND IN MY SHOE

Homestead Days
In Twentynine Palms

By Helen Bagley

With an Introduction by
LUCILE and HAROLD WEIGHT

Adobe Road Publishers
Twentynine Palms, California

First Printing 1978 Calico Press
Second Printing 1980 Homestead Publishers
Third Printing 1997 Adobe Road Publishers

Library of Congress Catalog Card No. 77-94990

International Standard Book Number 0-912714-08-5

Published by Adobe Road Publishers
P.O. Box 219
Twentynine Palms, California 92277
(760) 367-7726

Lithographed and bound in the United States of America by
The Caxton Printers, Ltd.
Caldwell, Idaho 83605
162706

TO FRANK

And to our sons

John   Alan   Denny

Acknowledgements

I wish to thank Doctor Edward Lincoln Smith and Mary and Theodore Hayes for their encouragement and suggestions: Mrs. Winnie Simms for typing my cluttered manuscript. I am grateful to Lucile and Harold Weight for professional advice and especially for expert preparation of the photographs used in this book.

I acknowledge indebtedness to my husband, Frank, for his stories, his help, and his patience.

Table of Contents

List of Illustrations

Introduction

By Lucile and Harold Weight

On the border between the Colorado and Mojave deserts lies a unique corridor. Starting from a deep cut through the Little San Bernardino mountains, north of Palm Springs, it climbs into Mojave Yucca and Joshua Tree country, then all but closes again between the Sheep Holes and the Monte Negros. About two-thirds east along this corridor is the natural oasis of Twentynine Palms.

When the first known white man came through, in the 1840s, he was following an Indian trail. The San Bernardino Base Line was surveyed through, close to the oasis, in 1855, and from then on sporadic visitors came. Gold finds lured miners in the 1870s, and thereafter the corridor saw lines of freight wagons and other mule and horse drawn vehicles. But most of this time Twentynine Palms oasis served only as a temporary haven for the freighters and gold seekers who went on into the hills, and for cattlemen who brought herds down from high pastures.

Then, in the 1920s, the first determined home seekers reached the oasis. It is this period that Helen Bagley's "Sand in My Shoe" so vividly reflects. The kind of life these new adventurers experienced from the 1920s to the 1940s is virtually unknown to today's Americans. Compacted between two World Wars and dominated by the great depression of the 1930s their existence in this then-remote desert oasis was a throwback to an earlier period. These pioneers had to start with nothing.

Their story, "Sand in my Shoe," is regional history as it should be written — not in dates, names and statistics, but in the ventures, adventures and misadventures of the people without whom there would be no history to record. There can be no question of the book's appeal to those who shared the experience, or of its special interest to the hundreds of thousands who now know Twentynine Palms as the site of the "world's largest" Marine Corps Base (five miles to the north), and as a favored route to the Colorado River playgrounds. But as a well-told chronicle of the eternal struggle of individuals against chance, adversity, and their own natures, its universality reaches far beyond its desert valley.

And especially interesting are these pioneers — veterans, prospectors, miners, and out-of-time frontiersmen looking for a last frontier — who seem to have included some of the most stubbornly individualistic individuals ever to attempt to build a community.

Perhaps the isolation and the financial lack and the problems of a dry and empty desert were the major reasons for the remarkable community that Twentynine Palms became. Not only were these people dependent on their own efforts to survive, they were almost equally dependent in many ways upon their neighbors. Twentynine Palms' few voters made little impact on officials at the county seat, almost a hundred miles away, which meant they received little government help in their larger problems.

"As a community we were many kinds and of many minds," writes Helen Bagley. "Inevitably we disagreed. We did not work in peace and harmony. (But) sincerity, interest and enthusiasm we had in common. We accomplished."

Helen and Frank Bagley came to Twentynine Palms in 1927 with three small children — one a baby. They built a garage in which to live while they built a home and then a store. But with no store nearer than sixty miles — most of those miles a wandering sandy two-rut track — plans changed. The garage quickly became both store and home. The "store" was a few shelves in a corner, and the double bed had to be rolled outside before the business could operate. The last visitor-customer had to be shooed out before the family could sleep. And this became more complicated as "Bagley's" rapidly evolved into an unofficial community center.

From this vantage (and sometimes disadvantage) point
Helen Bagley saw and took part in the growth of Twentynine Palms for more than forty years. All the varied dwellers of the region became familiars. And she saw them not
as just customers but as individuals whose strength and
weaknesses, delights and disappointments and sorrows she
understood and shared. Her vignettes of their lives and the
life of Twentynine Palms, written with gentle empathy and
a wry, understated humor will not soon be forgotten. The
pioneers of Twentynine Palms not only had sand in their
shoes — they had grit where it was needed.

To the Pioneers

By Helen Bagley

This region has been Indian Country, prospected and mined, used as open range for cattle. Then came the homesteaders. They used to have a saying, "Uncle Sam bets you 160 acres of sand that you can't live on it for three years without starving to death." In early years few who filed remained to make a home.

After the war, in the Twenties, there was an increase in homesteading. Frank and I came in 1927. We estimated that there were from fifty to one hundred such settlers from Yucca Valley to the Dale Mining Region. Many of these were veterans of World War I and some had been sent here by Dr. James B. Luckie. He knew this generation of veterans, for he was one of them.

Many were disabled by asthma, T.B. or had lungs burned by mustard gas. He traveled the deserts to find a climate that would help them. He wanted about two thousand feet elevation, pure water, warm and sunny air. He found them here. Dr. Luckie began to tell his patients, "Go out to Twentynine Palms and file on a homestead."

When we came here we drove over a winding road, worn and rutted by the wagons that had carried supplies to the mines. There was not one mile of straight road. There was no group of buildings that could be called a village; no post office, store or school.

But there came a corps of homesteaders who wanted homes on land they owned and a background of sound community life.

Most were poor, but they worked together. They shared. They shared water, they nursed and helped each other in trouble. Shared too the joys, had fun in homespun ways. They rejoiced in the challenge of frontier living, in wilderness, in wide spaces and the stars.

After the school was built they worked on roads. Women helped, pulling and burning brush, bringing food at lunch time. Children thought it a treat to ride the drags to smooth the cleared roads.

Soon there were miles of cleared road, where two cars could pass without one having to pull off and get stuck in the sand.

There is a verse which expresses our efforts —

> "Neighbors lend a hand
> And sort of pass themselves around
> Out in the desert land."

The homesteaders still had a long way to go and a rough road to travel. Not everyone worked, and they had not agreed, but they had accomplished. There was a new sense of confidence and pride.

Working together they formed close ties and lasting friendships. It was not only the clear air and the sunshine that healed the body and gave new spirit. Life was worth living.

There are still a few with us who worked in those days, and have continued to contribute through nearly half a century, to the town of Twentynine Palms.

> — From an Address accepting the Twentynine Palms Pioneer Memorial, on behalf of the Pioneers of the 'Twenties, at the Dedication on October 17, 1976

Homestead

Jim Travers had a homestead,
    A square half mile of land,
The desert stretched on every side
    With greasewood, sage and sand.

Jim Travers had a homestead,
    And not much else beside,
But a shack a man has made himself
    Can fill his heart with pride.

He had no need of many things,
    He didn't wear a shirt,
He hauled his water in a can;
    Clean sand is not like dirt.

Boiled beans will fill a belly up
    With salt pork for a treat.
He had a rabbit now and then,
    Or turtle for fresh meat.

He worked for wages when he could,
    But neighbors lend a hand
And sort of pass themselves around
    Out in this desert land.

The air was sparkling clear and clean,
    The sun was hot at noon.
Red sunset blazed across the sky,
    Came dusk, and then the moon.

HOMESTEAD

Bare mountains fifty miles away
    Shone white beneath its light.
Jim slept beneath the vast round sky.
    He loved the desert night.

The desert's wealth is for the poor,
    Alone-ness without bars;
Aloneness in a friendly land;
    Wide spaces and the stars.

Jim Travers had the sort of wealth
    That comes where lands are wide,
Jim Travers had a homestead —
    And not much else beside.

I. An Adventure in Living

Homestead Store

We saw Twentynine Palms in the spring of 1927. We had driven from the highway at Whitewater across a single track road which dodged Joshua trees, boulders, even greasewood bushes. When we chose the site for our homestead and store, a few months later, we reached it across untracked sand.

There was not even a mile of straight road. More important, there was no school, post office, or store. The Gold Park Hotel, then east of the Oasis of Mara, sold groceries from its stock, when they could be spared, and gasoline, to homesteaders who had "run out." No group of buildings could be called a village. A population of from fifty to one hundred persons was scattered from Yucca Valley to the Dale mining district and from the dry lake to the Oasis. There was a cattle ranch near Yucca Valley and a few prospectors in the hills. Most of the settlers were homesteaders, and many of them were veterans of World War I. It was a frontier community.

My husband, Frank, had heard of the settlement in Twentynine Palms through other veterans in Pasadena. For several years he had been having asthma. In the fall of 1927, desperate from ill health, he decided to move to the desert. He filed on a homestead and put up our first building, designed for a double garage. In November he brought the family out. John, our eldest son was six, Alan three, and Denny only four months old.

We had promised ourselves that although the desert might hold some hardships, we would enjoy a sense of limitless space, quiet, and peace. We were to find that these are not easily realized in a double garage with three children and a grocery store.

My first impression of my new home was of the kindness
of my neighbors, and not of loneliness. Jim Byler, who lived
on a homestead a mile from ours, our next door neighbor
by desert standard, had driven our pickup from Pasadena
with furniture while Frank followed with the family. During
the hour by which Jim had preceded us he had managed to
unload, put our rug on the floor and set up our beds, giving the place somewhat the look of home. I put the baby
down from aching arms and thanked him. He grunted,
glanced from me to my old bureau with its large mirror,
and said shortly:

"You fixing to be a lady?" He strode out.

Jim had been in the American Expeditionary Force at
sixteen, and in and out of hospitals ever since. He tried
hard, but not quite successfully, to live down a family background of gentle ways.

Our building had been intended only as a garage. It had
a cement floor and apron in front, was lined with black
building paper, unfinished as to beams and ceiling. It had
been our plan to have a small house with a large front room
to be used as a store, an arrangement common then in any
rural community. But the truck and garage had cost more
than we expected, and the right of entry on our land was
clouded by a previous lease. We had not much money left
from doctor bills, and so we decided to move into the
garage building and wait for the store.

We could at least set up a gas pump and enjoy whatever
business and income that might bring us. Frank hired Bill
Smith to help him. Bill was round-shouldered, with the
walk of one who followed the plow too early. He had "accidentally" come to the desert and remained to homestead.
He intended to farm someday; there was no hurry.

The single gas pump was placed in position near the
corner of our garage house. The two men, using a hand
mixer, were about to mix the cement for the foundation
when a woman drove up in an old Packard car.

"Bill," she drawled in a soft southern voice, "you promised to locate me a homestead. Ah want you should come now."

Bill sat back on his heels and considered. "Wal, I sort of hired out to Frank to set this here pump."

"Ah certainly never yet saw any homesteader in a hurry."

Bill considered. Certainly in the fifty miles of desert we could see from our hill there was no line of cars waiting for a service station. He climbed into the Packard. "I might accidentally get back tonight," he reassured us.

It was a two man job. I had been watching with the baby in my arms; I carried him to his bed in the building. "I can turn the mixer while you pour," I said.

Then Bob McCown came along. McCown was a lunger who had left the terminal ward of a veteran's hospital by the front door because he, and everyone else, was tired of waiting for him to leave by the back. The three of us set the pump.

It was Thanksgiving day. We had boiled beans and canned spinach for dinner. But we were grateful. We had made a beginning.

Our garage house seemed well occupied with the five of us living in it. The right hand side of the room was our kitchen. There was a long table with a window and two shelves for groceries above it. Our stove was a two burner gasoline camp stove, later replaced by a little wood range in the corner.

At the back was a single bed in which the two boys slept, end to end. This was not a congenial arrangement. The cry, "Mama, Johnny's touching me," came to be a byword in our family. The baby slept in his carriage.

The corner was curtained with black, brightly flowered chintz, and beside it stood the old bureau with the large mirror to which Jim Byler had objected. One top drawer held the office equipment for the gas station. The cash was kept in a cigar box. When we thought to replace the box with a muffin tin for change, that was our first step toward modernization.

The curtained closet, the old bureau, and an army foot locker held all our clothing. We were not cursed with possessions.

I had only one decorative thing, and even it could be useful. A double brass candle sconce which I had bought in a dark Russian shop under the Second Avenue El in New York City, hung on our wall, bright against the black paper, near the chintz curtain of the wardrobe. When I sat down to feed my baby I faced that corner of the room. There was beauty, and after all one can enjoy the contemplation of only one beautiful thing at a time.

Our double bed — that was the complicating factor of our lives. The only possible place for it was the middle of the room. In the morning it was made up immediately and pushed out through the double doors onto the apron of the building. The arrangement was adequate unless it should rain. This was the desert. It was not supposed to rain.

The shelves above the work table openly displayed our household stock of cans and packages, and the way of the frontier was a general and generous sharing of supplies. When food ran low neighbors borrowed. People knew we planned to have a store and our groceries were in plain view. Nothing was more natural than that they should buy or borrow of us.

Gas station customers had bought our last loaf of bread. I made biscuits and they were good. But when I was busy with the baby the middlesized boy ate too many. His stomach "bounced " as he said, all day and all night.

I said, "Frank, if we are going to have proper food for ourselves and keep people's goodwill we will have to open our store."

"How can we, in this place?"

"There is nothing essential in that corner by the door," I pointed out.

And so he built four five-foot shelves in the corner, and I made a list of groceries for our initial stock, keeping carefully in mind that if no one bought things we would eat them. A few cases and half cases of tinned meats and vegetables, a few bunches of carrots, cabbage and potatoes, two sides of bacon.

The nearest town was Banning, sixty miles away, and fifty of it over the old single track dirt road. But for wholesale supplies Frank must go to Riverside, one hundred miles distant. A man in a truck could make the round trip in a day if nothing went wrong.

Frank left at daybreak, promising to be home in time for the before-supper trade. Sunset came, and gas customers. I learned to test for oil in a Model T where one crawled half way under the car. People waited around for a while hoping for their bread and bacon. They left. I put the children to bed and listened to the coyotes. At last I put Frank's Army forty-five automatic under my pillow and went to bed. It was comforting, something like having a telephone.

The automatic made a lump; I moved it under the vacant pillow, but I could not sleep.

"How come?" I asked myself. "How come I am lying here in a double garage away out in the Mojave desert with a 45 Colt under a vacant pillow?" Perhaps it would help to remember.

I remembered that the first thing I had noticed about Frank was the way he rode a bicycle, upright, his head high, his hands barely touching the handle bars. We were both going to the Academy of Willamette University in Salem, Oregon. The Statehouse and the Courthouse there have a long narrow park running for several blocks through the center of the city. Willamette University is on one side of the park. My home, a comfortable welcoming sort of house, was on the other side. I walked across the park to classes, and Frank rode his bicycle there. After our acquaintance had progressed we used to walk together in the evening under the arching Maple trees, and he told me how he happened to ride a bicycle with such style.

His first job, when he had gone to work as a messenger boy at fourteen, had been carrying trays of food from restaurants to public houses, through the traffic of city streets in Spokane. There had been a fitted cap for his head; the tray placed on that. He had never dropped one.

Later he had found work in a hardware store. It paid twenty-five dollars a month, which was about standard for a boy during the hard times of 1907. He walked the three miles to his work, although carfare was five cents, and in the winter he often ran because he did not have an overcoat. When he got home he was expected to wait on, and shave, his grandfather who was one hundred years old, and blind, and who often, by way of conversation called him by his father's name. "Hoddie, do you remember that election in 1875? Who was it that won?"

Frank turned his pay check over to an older sister who managed for four of them on that amount. He told me that although he had been always hungry, and often cold, he had thought of it only as being the usual thing.

His father once had owned a large wheat ranch with two complete harvesting and threshing outfits with the appropriate complement of horses. He had sold out and moved to the city, trying to save his wife's life. She had died of cancer when Frank was twelve. His father had returned to the area where he was known and tried to establish himself in business, leaving the older daughter and one younger than Frank with their grandfather in a borrowed house in Spokane.

When Frank was eighteen, working as a bank clerk, he realized that although he was faster and more accurate than other boys (who often asked him for help) they would be advanced and he would not. They had college degrees. When after two years it became possible to leave the household he came to Willamette University. Because he was twenty years old he was rated as a special student and could take work in either the academy or college.

Strong, well coordinated, his bearing quiet but confident, he always found jobs. He was dark with deep set grey eyes. I thought he was handsome. At fifteen I lost all interest in boys my age.

That first year he worked as a night guard at the

Oregon State Penitentiary. This left daylight hours for classes, odd minutes for study. In summer he was assigned to walk the high wall of the brickyard, a rifle always over his shoulder. This was not advancement or what he wanted of life. He bought a volume of poetry, cut out the pages. Folded small, a page could be carried hidden against the butt of his rifle. He memorized well.

Now when we walked on summer evenings, he would quote Shakespeare, Burns, Bryant.

He had other jobs. For a time, to save rent, he was call boy at a fire station, sleeping in the loft and sliding down a pole to jump on the wagon when there was an alarm. He loved athletics and managed to find time for basketball and track. When the school had a decathlon he won easily.

In the summer of 1917 the call for volunteers for the "war to end all wars" was urgent. "Uncle Sam Needs You." Frank wanted to serve — but not to kill. He enlisted in a Base Hospital unit, then felt that was not enough. With difficulty he managed to transfer to the Air Corps.

We had been engaged for two years. When he won his wings and his commission we wanted to marry. My parents urged us to wait but they would not refuse permission. They went with me to meet him. We were married in Albuquerque, New Mexico, in a church with my father and mother as witnesses.

When Frank reported back to his Base he was assigned to a small field in Mississippi to instruct in "stunt flying" giving refresher courses to other officers who had already graduated. Stunt flying it was called. It was in reality the defensive maneuvers of single combat. These pilots flew Jennies, bi-planes with maximum speed of about seventy miles an hour. They had no parachutes.

So much to remember — I was about to fall asleep there in the garage. I murmured to myself, "to be continued in our next — " Then the baby woke. I looked at my clock with a flashlight. It was two o'clock. I rose and fed and comforted him. John sat up in bed. "Is daddy back?"

"He will be soon, John. Go to sleep again."

Alan mumbled from the other end of the single bed, "Mama, Johnny's touching me."

Such little tikes! What had I done bringing them here? Three o'clock now. Had Frank had an accident on the rough and lonely road? I was wide awake again. Better to go on with my story than to lie there being frightened by imagining.

I had been remembering romance. It had led me here to a garage in the Mojave desert with three small boys.

Frank and I had been married one month when he brought me his overseas orders. He said, "Smile," and handed them to me to read. He was to report at Hoboken, an embarkation point, on November 14, 1918. I went along.

The day we arrived in New York the city was wild with joy. The early false report of the Armistice had come in. We said the celebration was for us. On the night of the true Armistice, the eleventh, we had gone to a theater on Broadway. The street had been closed to traffic. It was a solid mass of people walking, shouting and singing with joy. Police, stolid but smiling, lined the sides of the street, watchful but not interfering. Many in the crowd were men in uniform. They were being greeted as heroes of the peace.

Frank and I thought it would be interesting to live in New York for a year or so. When he received notice that he would be discharged he went to a small bank in Columbus Circle to apply for a job. He went directly to the president of the bank who was an abrupt, gruff man. He looked Frank up and down. (Frank was still in uniform.)

"Where did you ever work in a bank?"

Frank told him the names of banks in Portland and Salem, Oregon.

"What did you do there?"

"I was a receiving teller."

The president called to the cashier. "Mr. Howe, give this man a job. Put him all through the bank. Give him any salary he wants."

Frank soon found out why. There were few in that bank

who even looked like bank clerks. Men eligible for military service had enlisted, so Mr. Howe had been managing with girls and ex-policemen. Frank had some difficulty in learning to understand Brooklynese. "Sure, I live at a hunt toity toid street."

Frank was started in a teller's cage, but the bank was expanding. He served as manager of a bond department, and then a new business department. Life was bright.

I was enjoying the city. I explored, found free concerts at odd hours, took long rides on top of buses, down Riverside Drive or Fifth Avenue to Washington Square. We lived near Columbia University and I entered classes. That night in the garage I gratefully recalled that one of my courses had been home nursing. Casually I wondered if I should have studied typing and bookkeeping.

After our son John was born I had less liberty. But the first day I wheeled him out in his carriage I met more friendly neighbors than in the three years before.

But Frank was not well. In Texas where he had trained he had begun having asthma. He would wheeze desperately at night but it did not interfere with his work in daytime. When he went to the camp doctor he was given the routine prescription, castor oil. Few soldiers went back a second time. Now he was worse; he had to be careful not to wheeze at the bank.

We had always intended to return to the West. Now with Frank's problem and a child to think of we decided to go to California. I thought, "How smart we are just to make up our minds where we want to live and go there."

So we moved to Pasadena, a beautiful sunny city, full of trees and flowers. The vegetation was a curse to Frank. He readily found a job in a bank. But he learned that so many people from the East had come, as we had for the beauty of the town, that they were not expected to require a living wage.

Alan and Denny were born there. We needed to manage on about half the salary Frank had received in New York.

At night before I went to bed I would arrange the dining table for Frank. I would put out a blanket on a chair, a deck of cards, a magazine. When he could not lie down and breathe he would get up and sit there, leaning over, his head on his hands, fighting for air. Often when he dressed for work I had to kneel and tie his shoes for him. He could not bend down to do it. Then he would go to the bank, stand in a cage all day, trying not to breathe hard, being courteous and efficient. He was unusually accurate in his work and had shown initiative in employee affairs. He was well regarded.

Sick though he was, even there, he had found some outlet for his ability in civic affairs. He had been active in promotion of the first public golf course in Pasadena, and he had many friends in the American Legion Post 334. It was Ben Benioff, aware of Frank's struggle with asthma, who said, "Frank, I have a little cabin out in the desert. Why don't you come out and try it there?"

Frank accepted and spent a month in Ben's one room shack. The air was healing: he could breathe and he could sleep.

Bill Campbell, homesteading nearby, suggested, "Frank, we need a grocery store in Twentynine Palms. Why don't you start one?"

A grocery store? The fact that Frank did not know spinach from turnips seemed no reason to deter us. We thought anyone could run a grocery store. . . .

I must have fallen asleep for the next thing I knew it was daylight, and I heard the truck back up on the apron of the garage.

The truck had broken down. Frank had driven all night, knowing that I would worry. The truck repairs had cost him forty-five dollars. He had bought fifty dollars worth of groceries for stock. We priced them up 25%, thinking that was the proper margin on selling, and having decided we could do business on that. The truck, of course, must not break down again.

We would see, we would soon find out whether just anyone could run a grocery store.

"The Oasis was a welcome camping place."

"A road worn and rutted by horse-drawn vehicles freighting to mining camps."

We arranged the groceries on our four shelves, trying to make an impressive display. Our first customers gave us friendly advice:

"Don't you never start cutting a slab of bacon in the middle like folks will ask you to do. Start at one end and let us take it as it comes."

We were in business.

Two days later a boy asked Frank to give him a quart of gasoline to clean a part of his motor. Frank half filled a can and set it on the ground between them. The boy lit a cigarette and dropped the match. It fell into the open can. Flame shot up. The boy kicked the can in panic, spraying Frank from head to foot with blazing gasoline. The flames smothered him. He flung himself down, rubbing his face in the sand. He told me afterwards. "It felt comforting."

A man standing there snatched a blanket from our bed and threw it over Frank, extinguishing the flames.

The boy who had kicked the can took off. The man helped me bring Frank into the building and then he left.

I tried to clean the sand from the burns with oil and cotton. Frank's arms and legs had been burned through his clothing. His face was seared and stuck full of coarse sand. We got his clothes half off. He was jittery with shock and sure that anything I could do would be wrong.

Fortunately there appeared in our door a neighbor who had been a pharmacist. He was a shy man, deaf and nearly blind. All that he could see was that Frank was half undressed and that I was on my knees in front of him.

"Do come in," I cried.

"No, no, thank you," he demurred. "I was just going to get some bread, but wouldn't wish to intrude."

"We need you. Please come in."

"Oh, thank you very much," he said politely. "I'll come another day."

He turned to go. I jumped up, caught his arm and pulled him in where he could see. Between us we dressed the burns.

Everyone who came to the gas station that evening offered to help. Everyone except one old man. He was a lean cadaverous trapper from Tennessee and he was much annoyed that Frank would not be going to town the next day because Frank promised to take some skins to an agent for him. I was to recall that incident later.

Jim Byler came to haul our water and he insisted on making the next trip to town. Jim was very proud of his fast driving. He left at dawn, was back at midnight and the repair bill for the trip was only thirty-nine dollars and eight-seven cents.

To cheer us Jim made the boys a gift of two pups. They were of mixed but excellent ancestry. Their mother was Jim's fine black collie, their sire an intelligent Irish Water Spaniel which belonged to Bill Smith. The pups were black, curly, roly-poly, able to walk and run but too baby-clumsy to turn a corner without falling down.

The boys were delighted and loved them at once. Our baby, Denny, was charmed and entertained when they came close and barked at him, and three-year-old Alan felt that now his life lacked nothing. He could not tell them apart and he would call excitedly, "Mother, come look. The other pup is fighting th' other one!" We named them Mike and Ike because "Mike and Ike, they look alike."

To celebrate the fact that we were all related in a way, and to show appreciation of their kindness, we invited Jim and Bill for dinner. To my consternation they arrived at four-thirty. The main course was a leg of lamb which Jim had brought from town. That was a very special treat and dinner could not be hurried.

It was quite a party! Frank's face and hands were still done up in boric compresses; he looked as though he had the mumps, and his arms were so stiff and sore he could scarcely manage eating. Jim and Bill wore clean bib overalls and white shirts. They insisted they were entirely comfortable sitting side by side on a saw horse but they left immediately after eating. A seat on a saw horse does not conduce to lingering over coffee and cigarettes.

What remained of that leg of lamb would have served us

for several days. But sometimes my household arrangements became confused. The next morning, in order to bathe the baby on the kitchen table, I set the pan with the leg of lamb in it under the table. Then there were customers at the gas pump. When I came in Mike and Ike were so stuffed they could not walk even a straight line without falling down.

We entertained Veda Worrel and Ben Benioff with a dinner of jack rabbit cooked in tomato soup. It was Ben who had invited Frank to stay in his cabin and try the effects of the climate. He was a serious young veteran who had graduated from Cal Tech only to be ordered to the desert to clear up incipient tuberculosis. Veda was a kindergarten teacher, recuperating from major surgery. They were good to us, and our children loved them.

Veda and Ben were falling in love and their happiness seemed to create a glow in our dingy room.

It was time for more supplies. The bandages were off Frank's face and he thought that he was able to make the trip. He left in the late afternoon planning to stay overnight in Riverside.

Driving the crooked single track road to the west with the sun in his eyes he saw too late, a small truck speeding toward him. Just where they would meet, a hump of ground with a big Joshua tree was on Frank's right. Both trucks turned out on the same side of the road. Ours was heavier. The little truck, loaded with baled hay, shuddered to the ground.

Both drivers leaped out, unhurt, and walked around surveying the damage. The driver of the pickup was a well set-up dark man, his dress complete with cartridge belt and gun. He said nothing. Our Franklin truck had a crushed running board. His light truck was a complete wreck. The man with the gun began visibly to bristle. His face flushed beneath the tan, his eyes grew blacker. Frank thought it time to say something.

"I'm Frank Bagley of Twentynine Palms."

"I'm Bill Keys."

Frank pulled his hat down hard. He had the feeling that his hair was about to stand on end. Bill Keys was known as a man who made his own laws. Rumor had it that there were notches on his gun. He was not a man to be lightly crossed — let alone run into. That old Model T, successor to the burro in the Mojave, was his transportation, and he lived twenty miles from even that crooked road up in the mountainous country. He was growing madder minute by minute as he realized the extent of the damage. His cheeks began to quiver.

Frank told himself, "You had better do something and quick!"

"Mr. Keys," he said, "you come here. I have something to show you. Look through my windshield." Keys came, and through the dirty windshield he could see little but the setting sun's glare.

"Now," said Frank, "that is why I couldn't see you. But why in hell didn't you see me?"

"You are right, Mr. Bagley," said the man with the gun. "I had my mind on some mining deals. I should have seen you."

The Franklin would run. Together the men moved the bales of hay into it and Frank turned around and drove Bill Keys to his home.

Keys' Ranch lies in the mountains above Rattlesnake Canyon, half hidden among giant boulders. Prospecting with burro and pick, Keys found something better than gold. He had come by way of Death Valley, a wandering man. He took root like the piñon pines. He built a dam between boulders which raised the level of a natural reservoir and held water from the winter snows. In a cove sheltered from the fiercest heat and winds he built a house, planted an apple orchard and established a family.

In this remote stronghold Frank was received graciously by a woman with a complexion as delicate as apple blossoms. There were three children about the ages of ours. Mrs. Keys listened to her husband's account of the collision without rancor, accepting his judgment of shared blame.

"It's a bad road to travel," she said, "because not many do. And you don't expect to meet another one like yourself." She gave them dinner and made room for Frank to sleep.

The next day the men went to Riverside. Frank told Bill to buy another car as good as the one just wrecked and he would pay for it because he had been wrong in turning left.

Frank put his own truck in a garage. It had suffered more damage than he realized. It was second-hand. He had ordered it rebuilt to his design especially for hauling groceries. Later he learned that it had been put together from three wrecked vehicles. It was air cooled and had a heavy tubular frame, but the rough roads shook it apart.

The third day Frank divided his time between the garage and shopping for our five grocery shelves. His arms were paining him but he ignored the pain. There was too much else to worry about.

At day's end he found Bill Keys again. "How have you come out?"

"Frank, I found another pickup."

"Is it satisfactory? And how much was it?"

"Oh yes," said Bill, "it is even a little better than the one I had. But . . . it cost twenty-five dollars."

Frank wanted to pay for his hotel room but Bill refused to accept anything more than the price of the truck. The old truck, he said, had cost fifty dollars but he had driven it five years.

Late that night Frank reached home with his load. He was exhausted, wheezing with asthma, and the pain in his arms was intense. Driving in the dark he had examined them; there was a chain of lumps, like beads, up the veins inside his elbows and in his armpits. And when he finally opened the garage door, longing for rest, there was not even a place to sleep.

While he was away, Veda, who was a guest at the Gold Park Hotel, concerned about me and my problems with babies and business, had come to help me. There had been no message from Frank because there was no phone. When night came and we pushed the double bed inside, she stayed, sharing my bed.

Frank said, "Don't get up, Veda. I'll go to the hotel and come back in the morning to unload."

It was a fortunate circumstance that sent him there. Frances Roberts, who ran the Inn, was a trained nurse. She had only to see Frank to know that he was ill. "Oh my God, Frank," she exclaimed, "you have blood poisoning! You can't stay here tonight. You must get to a doctor at once."

Frank knew that he was in no condition to drive back to the city. The nearest doctor was in Banning, sixty miles away. But he had a friend. He went to the home of Bill Campbell and knocked. Bill and his wife Betty came to the door together. Frank told his story and asked Bill if he would take him into Banning.

Bill said, "Sure, Frank . . ."

Betty broke in. "You will do no such thing! Bill, you draw a warm bath for this man and put him to bed. He must have rest." To Frank she said, "I know something about burns. I nursed after that big ammunition explosion in New Jersey. My husband will take you to a doctor in the morning. But rest must come first."

In the morning Frank was back at our garage-store-nursery. The truck had been unloaded into the middle of the room. He handed me the bills so I could price the stock.

For the trip they were:

Truck repairs	$59.50
Gas and oil	6.25
Pickup for Mr. Keys	25.00
Stock for store	49.00

Bill Campbell came to get Frank. He looked in and saw Veda, me and the children surrounded by crates of produce and boxes of cans. I suppose it looked dismal. In the kindest way he said:

"I left a fire on the hearth for my wife. If time hangs heavy on your hands go down and sit with her."

If Time Hung Heavy

If time hung heavy on our hands! We used it as a joke to cheer ourselves when things were hard. For the simple life is not always simple.

But Frank's burns did heal. Dr. Cook of Banning told him that he had no doubt that Betty's treatment with a night of rest and fresh poultices of antiseptic had saved his life.

And we were getting things organized. A desert cooler outside our building kept vegetables fresh, and during the cold months it would keep pasteurized milk for a few days. This cooler was built of heavy wire, covered with burlap. A galvanized wash tub on top had perforations to let the water drip gradually down the sides. We had no other refrigeration so meat was brought only on order.

All our first stock of groceries was contained in our four five foot shelves. Besides food we carried ammunition, nails, water bags and gas cans.

Our stock grew on demand. One of our early customers was a miner; he had driven twenty miles to the store and he asked for matches.

Frank and I looked at each other in consternation. Neither of us had thought of them. "What the hell kind of a store is this?" stormed our prospect. We gave him nearly all our own. The next week our emporium carried matches.

When Frank went to town I had to wait on customers and try to keep my nursery in the background. In the afternoons I could manage fairly well. Alan, my three year old, took a nap in the back seat of the car. Denny napped in his carriage which was pushed far enough from the building so that his sleep was not disturbed. John, six, tried to be helpful. Poor little eldest son! We thought of him as almost grown.

Al Northey had been coming into the store for several weeks before he remarked in surprise, "Why, Mrs. Bagley. I never noticed you had a baby." But he would keep an eye on my cooking while he shopped.

He was a little man with a big gun strapped on him and an extra belt of ammunition draped around his neck. He said his name of "Al" was short for alcohol because he took it straight. A spotted dog, trained to be vicious, was with him in his car. Al told me this was because his life had been threatened. He seemed to be very proud of having had his life threatened.

"There is too much law and not enough Winchester law in this country, Mrs. Bagley," he would say. And then, "Your carrots need more water." While I put up his order he watched my stove.

The widow who owned the Packard and the southern drawl used to pick up my baby while I waited on her. She had once run a similar store in her front room with a child of an age to fall into the sugar barrel.

That Packard, by the way, was our best customer for a time. It required a gallon of oil a day until Frank repaired it. He was like that.

On days when Frank was away, five in the afternoon was my zero hour — the hour of flaming sunsets, when the Sheep Hole Mountains change to mauve and gold and brooding peace descends upon the desert. The children were tired and wanted supper. The baby wept and refused to be comforted. Wood and water must be brought inside before dark; the gasoline lanterns, which frightened me, must be lit just so.

And there were the customers, more than at any other time of day, stopping on their way home. I tried to solve the problem by waiting on the store with the baby on my hip, but I was likely to add wrong. And I could not learn to service a car and tote the baby.

I tried to teach the six year old to do a big boy's work, to

bring in wood and soothe the baby. I tried to be bright and
pleasant and think that a liberal arts education should prepare one to wait on a grocery store and manage a hungry
infant with smoothness and efficiency. It just remained a
zero hour.

Knowing that we did not have enough money to carry
charge accounts, Frank and I had determined not to give
credit. My first credit sale occurred at half-past zero hour.

The regular customers had gone and sitting down at last
I had begun to nurse my baby. A truck drove up to the gas
station. I put the baby on the bed and went out with my
brightest customer manner. The old couple in the truck
were less friendly than most: I think they considered us
bourgeois. They asked for five gallons of motor oil and I
had only a quart measure. Four times five is twenty. It was
so cold that it took a minute for the oil to run into the quart
can and out again. During all that time my poor frustrated
infant wept until he was reduced to hysterical sobs. John
was too small to lift or carry him, and no six year old could
have diverted for long a hungry baby who wanted his
mother. Twice I went inside and moved him with my oily
hands so that he could not throw himself off the bed on to
the cement floor.

All this time the old people sat patiently and compla-
cently while I measured oil. I comforted myself with the
thought of how badly we needed the money from that sale.

"This will be $9.00," I informed them.

"Just charge it," said the man. "Charge it to McCown.
He owes us money and he said this would be okay."

It was some time before I could think that sale was
funny. But most of it was fun and when things were very
hard they had to be funny.

One day a fragile little woman with big eyes, Mrs. Iva
Hill, sat in my kitchen corner and looked at my cement
floor and bright congoleum rug, the black building paper
showing between the studs of the walls and my good cook
stove. She said, "You certainly have things nice here. I have
no floor and the rabbits burrow in."

After that I never thought I was roughing it.

Hauling water was not a hardship. Frank had bought two fifty gallon Coca Cola barrels, each fitted with a spigot at the bottom. The barrels were hauled upright on our truck, then tilted and rolled gently on to a sturdy bench which had been built to the height of the truck bed and stood just in front of the building. So I had had running water at my door and I used it freely by desert standards. One barrel was sufficient for a day other than the weekly wash day. It supplied the tub above the desert cooler and enough water for baths, kitchen use, and the baby's daily wash.

Rolling the barrels from truck to bench was work for a strong man, but going after water was an idyllic interval in the day. We hauled our water from Bill Smith's place. He had a windmill and a five hundred gallon tank. It was not an adequate supply but desert tradition required that water be shared.

There was a true tale about the local meanest man. One day when the wind was not blowing he drained the tank so dry that Bill could not even make coffee, and then he complained that there had not been enough to fill his barrel.

Bill lived alone and he was seldom at home in the day time. The quiet of his place, the spot of green grass, the athol trees high above his cabin, the whir of the windmill wheel and the chug of the rod pumping in the well; these brought a spell of enchantment and peace in the arid wideness of the desert. The water ran slowly so that for twenty beautiful minutes there was nothing to do but rest, listen to the wind in the trees, listen to the water, and rest.

We bathed there too, under the water from the hose, being careful that the water ran onto the little alfalfa patch or the trees. There is nothing more exhilerating than a bath under the desert sun, — unless it be under the desert moon.

The solitude of space assured privacy. Only once I had a narrow escape. I had stripped, rinsed, generously soaped myself from head to foot with fragrant lather and was about to rinse again when a car came into view a hundred yards away. There was just time to put on my print dress over the soap when the driver pulled in for water. I chatted a moment with what I hoped was perfect poise while the soap dried on my body.

"Good morning, Mr. Pennell." (I was glad he was old enough to be nearsighted.) "It's a lovely day, isn't it?"

"Just came from your store. I see you had the baby's laundry out already. It certainly is good weather for drying things."

"Yes, that's one good thing about this country." I was trying not to squirm.

"I've been wanting to tell you, Mrs. Bagley, it seems good to see a baby's washing out here in the desert."

This struck me as an astonishing and novel idea for I had been hanging out children's clothes daily for more than six years. "Well, thank you, Mr. Pennell. It's nice to know someone feels that way." For a moment I forgot the soap. "Yes," I said, stupidly, "it is wonderful weather for drying things."

After polite goodbys I drove home, waited until there were no customers in the store and washed off the soap in our tin basin.

One evening when Frank was away, Bill Smith came bringing two barrels of water. Veda was with me that evening; it was a pleasant and relaxed time. The children were settled in bed, the dishes washed and put away. We had been talking, Veda and I, of what we might be doing if we were in the city; a trip to the library for new books, perhaps, or going to the latest show.

When Bill arrived with the water, we naturally went outside to greet him and watch him unload the barrels. These were fifty gallons each; the water alone weighed four hundred pounds. From our truck they could have been tilted and rolled onto the water bench, but Bill's truck was six inches higher. He carefully worked the barrel to the very edge then grasped it in his arms and lifted. It slipped and fell. As it fell the top came off and fifty gallons of water ran across the porch and poured into the store.

Chagrined, Bill took the second barrel and tried to edge it off more gently. It too fell and fifty more gallons flooded into the store. Bill said, "There might accidentally be enough water in my tank to bring you some more." He drove off.

"Accidentally," as Bill would have said, the floor of the building sloped in toward the back. Jim Byler and Bill had laid it for Frank. He had carefully instructed them to make it slope a little; it did, but the wrong way. We had kidded Bill about this and that probably added to his chagrin. But worse — Veda had seen him goof. Veda was young, a sunny, happy person, the only young woman within one hundred miles. Naturally, Bill would return.

Veda and I brought planks from the wood pile, took brooms and began sweeping the water out the wide front door.

It took Bill about thirty minutes to refill one barrel. He was back. This time he would lift that barrel. But now it was wet. Another fifty gallons of water ran into our store.

"Tell Frank I ain't agoing to charge him for this," Bill assured me.

We spent the evening mopping.

Our desert is beautiful; beautiful for wide spaces, for the mountains that rim our valley and change to rose, to violet, and then to mauve at sunset, for the vast sweep and glory of the stars at night.

Even our children responded as I had dared to hope. Alan was playing with pebbles in the sand in front of our building. There had not been room for toys when we moved out. He looked so small in the great space. My heart felt a pang.

"Do you like it here, Alan?"

He looked away at the distant horizon, "Oh yes," he said earnestly. "There are such pretty mountains."

Peace and solitude, these are the riches of the poor in a

desert land. And we were poor enough; but we were trying
to do something about it.

"Aren't you lonely in the desert? What do you do with
your time?" People from town asked these questions so
sympathetically.

Our day began when we heard the noise of a Model T
struggling up the hill on the old road from Mesquite Flats.
That would be our first customer, Fred Furniss, on his way
to work. We had just time to leap out of our bed in the
middle of the room, make it up and push it out the door.
We were dressed and ready to greet Fred when he arrived.

Fred had been a railroad man; he has a passion for time.
He worked for Bill Campbell, and had the only steady job
available. He would not be late. But Betty had admonished
him he must not be early. So he would stop at the store,
sometimes buy a can of Velvet tobacco and stand there looking at his watch until the moment he could leave to drive
two more miles and arrive at the exact minute, on schedule
for his work.

In spite of the fact that we lived in a grocery store we
had social life. Indeed, we had the more of it!

Meal times became an economic problem. What should
we do when a customer arrived just as our table was set for
a meal in the middle of the room? Hospitality demanded
that he be invited to eat with us. There was no excuse of
having just enough when I could always go to a shelf and
get another can.

Afterward we might hear, "Thank you very much. I
don't believe I need anything now." We had to make a rule
to wait on a customer before asking him to dinner.

It was best to put the little boys to bed as soon as possible
after supper. If we were alone I sang to them while I
washed the dishes, some melody of Stephen Foster's or:

> "Sleep my love, and peace attend thee
> All through the night."

Not that I could sing, but in that cluttered room, dimly lit with hissing gasoline lanterns, there was the more need of music. I wondered how long we might live that way. One night I heard Alan sleepily remark in that curiously deep voice of his, "Johnny, 'gone are the days when my heart was young and gay.' " I knew it was a line from "Old Black Joe" but because we were discouraged that night, it seemed more an omen than a joke.

Late in the evening some homesteader might come in to buy coffee and remain long hours to visit. Usually the baby slept. John and Alan would lie quietly watching from the shadows with eyes weighted by the sandman until they could watch no longer.

When the last friendly customer had gone, Frank would roll the bed inside, turn out all the lights and take his bath in the baby's tub. The Twentynine Palms Grocery and General Store closed for the night.

Peace and Prosperity

Christmas was a joyful day. Our tree was a piñon pine brought from the mountains near Keys' ranch. It was low and spreading, much too large for the room, but it filled our home with fragrance. John and Alan helped decorate it with popcorn, red apples, and paper chains. Frank and I gave ourselves to sharing their excitement. My family had sent a big box with toys and books for the boys. They had stuffed the corners with packages of tissue and rolls of toilet paper, just in case we had run out.

We went to the Gold Park Hotel for dinner. The dining room had been made festive with boughs of pine and juniper. There were red candles on the table and a red jello salad; after a month of dining in a gas station it seemed elegant.

In the afternoon we drove across the desert, exploring trackless ways. The boys watched for rabbits and for the little kit foxes that ran in front of our car and hid in the bushes to peer out at us. A grey coyote crossed and did not try to hide.

We drove east toward the Sheep Hole Mountains, watching their colors change. Storm clouds were gathering. The cumulus clouds were like castles, shining white. Miles away we saw the long frayed banners of the rain trailing from their parapets.

I had never thought of rain as a shower traveling with a drifting cloud. I had lived so long in Oregon and in cities without far horizons, rain had seemed to me to be just all around.

It was dark when we reached home. Coyotes were in full cry and thunder rumbled in challenge between the castled clouds. It had been a beautiful day. We loved the desert.

The next morning we woke to find that the rain had reached our hill and that it was, indeed, just all around. During the night water had run in under our garage-style doors and the floor was flooded. The water ran to the back under the children's beds; sweeping it out did not do much good. Frank put boards in front of my work table and when I stepped on them the water sloshed out over more of the floor. The Christmas tree was still up; the children could not bear to part with it. The double bed had to be kept inside. The drop leaf table was open for our meals and to serve as a counter in case we had customers. We did.

People came in for bread and bacon and for company. They edged around between the bed, the Christmas tree, the baby carriage and the table.

Frank muttered to me apologetically, "This is one hell of a mess!" I said, "Yesterday was wonderful." To myself I thought, "If we can be happy today we are pretty good."

Some customers spent the day. This complicated my child care problems. I could not push the baby carriage outside for Denny's nap, and he must be changed and fed as discreetly as possible. Late in the afternoon, holding him, I sat in the corner near the wood stove with my back turned to the public. I called Alan to stand beside me and kept him content with stories. John, who was six, naturally joined the men.

Jim and Bill Smith had been there for lunch and stayed on in spite of our remarks about the slope of the floor they had laid. Bob McCown came in later. They appeared to ignore my difficulties. Perhaps the bachelors rather enjoyed the domesticity; they seemed to be having a very good time.

Above the sound of my own low voice telling stories I heard snatches of their conversation. They talked of the roads and of the repairs of our truck, always more than the value of the stock Frank could bring in. And I heard Bill Smith suggesting, "I might accidentally haul your stuff on my truck."

If Frank did not have to make the trips to town there would not be those breakdowns and repairs. And when the sunset came, when the lanterns must be lit, the wood and water brought in, the children fed, customers waited on inside and at the service station, there would be two of us.

The garage room was still a mess: water on the floor, diapers drying behind the stove, the bed, the tree, the open table in the middle, people shopping and lingering to talk. But our little boys had enjoyed new toys and all the company; Denny had fallen asleep in my arms. We were warm; all day here had been goodwill and friendship about us. It had been another happy day.

Some time in January Bill Smith began to do our hauling. His truck was a flat bed and old, but Bill was gifted in the use of baling wire.

He had come to the desert to homestead four years before. On the drive from Whitewater his engine had stalled; he had broken his arm cranking it. He had arrived then, with a broken arm, an old truck and $1.34 capital. His boyhood had been spent on a Nebraska farm and he planned to make his land of value by raising alfalfa. He worked by the day and could do nearly anything that was wanted. He had acquired an eight by ten foot cook shack, a half enclosed feed shed in which he slept, a cow, a well, a windmill, and a tank. The ground around his place was always neat and clean. To be sociable or to relax he would sit on his heels, cowboy fashion, smoking cigarettes and carefully dropping the ashes into the turned up cuffs of his overalls. He worked as hard as anyone we knew and yet we always thought of him as sitting down.

Although it was in the winter that Bill began to make the trips for the store, he drove at night to keep his engine from over heating. He would leave on Thursday evening, arrive in Riverside about six in the morning. If he got tired he slept in the truck and he subsisted largely on pie and coffee. During the day he shopped for produce, meat, groceries and the "special orders," extra things customers wanted. When the markets closed he started home and he reached our store between nine and twelve. He wore his bib overalls and an old suit coat on even the most wintry nights "I ain't very cold," he said.

At first he also brought in the mail for Twentynine Palms from the post office at Whitewater. For some years it had been the custom that any responsible person might pick up the mail at Whitewater, the nearest post office, and leave it at the Gold Park Hotel (later known as the Twentynine Palms Inn). There it had been spread out on a table to be looked over as people came in. Since our trucker made regular trips, the mail was brought to the store.

The night the truck came in was a social occasion. If it was late most customers would leave but a few friends would wait, drinking cocoa and visiting until Bill arrived. They would help unload the truck and find their mail. Frank and I would unpack and arrange the stock. It was a struggle to read the pencilled invoices by the light of our flaring lanterns. We must snatch a few hours sleep before Saturday business began.

In the afternoon Bill would come back to settle up. For this business occasion the pocket of his bib overalls was always fastened with a safety pin. He would hand Frank all incidental items of expense and the cash invoices of special orders. He never had any written account, never wrote anything down himself. Frank would add up the charges, deduct the total from the amount Bill had taken in from the store and the checks he had cashed, and tell the result as, "You should have $3.45 left."

Bill would consider, "No," he might say, "I reckon not."

Frank would go over the slips again, once, twice more. Finally, with no word, Bill would unfasten the safety pin from his pocket and bring out the change, laying it on the table. Invariably he was correct.

Our simple life had become much simpler. We had been given an old tent, ten by fourteen, and had a good floor and screen sides built to fit it. We used it as a sleeping room. No longer did the double bed have to be pushed out

on the porch in the morning and the children could be put
to bed without waiting for customers to leave.

We could now have one wall of the garage building for
grocery shelves, all of eighteen feet. It was an astounding
and beautiful array of cans and packages. I used to sit and
admire it when the day's work was done.

There was a playpen for Denny in the middle of the
room. He learned to stand and push it when he was seven
months old, happily pulling things off the shelves. Stock
must be arranged with the little cans and light packages on
the shelves he might reach.

We continued to cook and eat in the store and after we
had the tent for sleeping the store hours became longer.
The place was a club of sorts. There was one customer who
had insomnia in the morning and another who had it at
night. They both dropped in to while away the hours.
Sometimes a miner or traveler stopped in the night to call
for his mail or ask directions. Frank usually made coffee or
cooked breakfast, no matter what the time.

We were enjoying a happy illusion of peace and pros-
perity. Our business ran about twenty dollars a day — even
seventy dollars on Saturdays. Of course, if even one customer went to town for a weekend all our careful calcula-
tions as to perishables might be upset. I sometimes stood
sadly by our window and watched a car drive by when it
should have turned down our road.

Credit, which we had promised ourselves not to give,
was already a problem. How can a small and friendly mer-
chant say no to a man who hopes to have money next
month — and is hungry now?

We were almost making a living. If business is good a
grocer can afford to eat. If business is bad he has to eat
things up.

One morning I was waiting on a prospector from the
hills. He said, "I told my partner I was agoin' to town."

I asked, "Are you going to San Bernardino?"

"No, I mean this town. Right here."

It was one of my proudest moments.

The Party

One peaceful evening in spring when we were about to close the store and go to bed we were called upon by Mrs. Potter, her two husky young sons and Jim Byler.

They had just returned from a hasty trip to Los Angeles and they wanted to buy ammunition. We had buckshot for the boys but not the cartridges Mrs. Potter wanted. "Don't you have any 38 police positives?" she demanded.

Jim asked to borrow Frank's 45 automatic. Frank lent it as a matter of course but the dour looks of the group made him curious.

"Are you going hunting tonight?" he asked. The silence that followed increased the tension. They filed out.

Jim was the last to leave. At the door he turned and muttered, "Skunk hunting."

I noticed lights burning in the valley toward Dead Man's dry lake, far into the night. For years afterwards lights in the night seemed sinister to me. For the events of that night and the weeks that followed; absurd, even comic, teetered above tragedy.

Ben Benioff came the next morning and told us the story.

After buying ammunition Mrs. Potter had driven to his cabin and then to Bill Smith's and roused them from bed. "Ah've had some trouble with a man down heah," she drawled, "and ah want to go down and talk things out. Ah want mah friends to go along and see that everything is fair."

Lillian Potter was the woman I have referred to as having the Packard and the Southern drawl. She kept her soft voice, a certain charm, and a fondness for other traditions of the South. The young men liked to drop in at her cabin near the dry lake for coffee and talk. She had been married five times but she spoke of herself as a widow, appealing to chivalry.

Both Ben and Bill were puzzled by her call, but willing to oblige a lady, they dressed and got into the car with Jim Byler.

Her sons stopped the car and picked up another boy, a pal of theirs. After a whispered conference he brought his shotgun. The boys then rode together in a jalopy.

The next stop was "Skeleton Ranch" where Al (short for alcohol) Northey and a cold-eyed Tennessean who had recently been appointed our deputy sheriff, joined the party. These men seemed to be expecting Mrs. Potter. Al came out buckling on his gun belt, a forty-five in the holster.

"There is too much law and not enough Winchester law in the country," he growled. He brought his dog, the spotted cur trained to be vicious. The deputy, whom we knew as a trapper, had a rifle and a Luger. Mrs. Potter was in the driver's seat of her car; the deputy climbed in beside her and held his rifle between his knees. Al got in next and they held the dog between them.

Ben and Bill, in the back seat, noticed that Jim was quivering. They alone were unarmed. "What's up anyway?" asked Ben. "Shut up and you'll find out," ordered Jim.

Over her shoulder Mrs. Potter said softly, "Ah need mah friends to help me settle a little matter that concerns mah honor."

The car was stopped near Fred Furniss' house. Mrs. Potter got out. "Mah sons and I will see to this part. You gen'lmen just stay in the car."

With her .38 in her hand, her sons, armed with shotguns on each side of her, she went to the door and called, "Fred, Ah want to talk to you a minute. Come on out."

Fred was in bed. He pulled on his trousers and some instinct warned him to take his gun. Standing inside his own door he demanded, "What do you want?"

"Ah want you to get into the car with mah friends. There's something ah want to talk to you about."

Fred had opened the door but held his gun in front of him. "I'm not coming until I know what's up."

"Boys," said Mrs. Potter, "you cover him with your shotguns. Ah'm going to take his gun."

Confronted with two shotguns trained at his middle Fred handed over his pistol.

He was taken to the car and the party went on a quarter of a mile to the house of Fred's father, Bob Furniss.

"What's up?" Fred kept asking.

"Shut up, you skunk," from Jim.

Al contributed, "We are going to settle this in the good ol' fashioned way."

Bill exclaimed, "I didn't come along on no murdering party!"

"You are going to keep still and take it, I'm the law here," from the deputy.

Bob Furniss came from his house when called. His white hair shone in the moonlight. He was surrounded by the three boys with shotguns. Al and Mrs. Potter produced from the car two old feather pillows and a can of something black and sticky. The lady pulled from under her seat a black snake whip and draped it like a scarf around her shoulders.

"Now gen'lmen," she said, "this old man, Bob Furniss, had been sayin' things that touch mah honor. Ah'm a widow and alone. Ah need the respect and sympathy of mah friends. Ah can't touch this old man because his hair is white and what Ah'm going to do might make him die. But he is going to watch.

"Boys, you keep him covered with your guns.

"Fred, Ah went all the way to Los Angeles today to get this black snake whip like we used to whip the niggers with where I came from." She pulled the long whip from her shoulders and drew it slowly through her hands. She dropped the soft drawl and her voice was harsh. "Ah'm going to whip you to the rind and then cover you with tar and feathers."

Bob Furniss protested. "I stay home and tend to my own business. Whatever do you think I said?"

"You told one of mah friends that any man who came to my house brought his reputation in his hands."

"No — never! I don't talk like that. I don't talk."

Ben went cold with anger. So this was what it meant "tar and feathers" — something he had read of in old history. To strip this decent man naked in front of all of them, to whip him raw, then to smear him with tar and cover him with feathers! And these excited eager men! He was careful to keep his voice even but he stated clearly, "I would as soon take the word of Bob Furniss as that of any man in this valley."

Al Northey said, "Let's get on with this. Let's settle it in the good old fashioned way."

Bill Smith had been getting madder by the minute. "I didn't come on no tar and featherin' party."

Al Northey said, "Well, you're in on one now."

"No," said Bill slowly, "I don't think I am." He took off his coat and threw it on the ground. "I'll fight you one at a time or all together. But I didn't come for no tar and feather party and I ain't going to stand here and watch."

Al, Jim, and the deputy drew off together and whispered. They had come for a spectacle, not for a fight. There was no bravado about Bill Smith. All his life he had worked hard and his muscles were like iron. So was his will. Together they might overpower him, but they would be hurt — and bad.

Mrs. Potter motioned to her boys to stay back and keep their shotguns on Fred Furniss.

Ben said, "Mrs. Potter, you asked us to come along and see that everything is fair. Bill doesn't seem to see it that way. Why not invite us to your house to talk things over?"

Jim Byler came around the Packard, picked up the tar and the feathers and put them in the car. Reluctantly, Mrs. Potter handed him the whip and he stowed that under the back seat.

Bill, still watchful, said slowly, "Lil, would you accidentally have some coffee there?"

They left Fred and Bob Furniss standing in the dark. They all drove to Lillian Potter's house, drank coffee and talked. Before they broke up, about daylight, the widow made her threat: "If any man talks against me Ah'll fill him full of lead. And if any woman besmirches mah name, Ah'll slit her tongue."

The men and boys of the "tar and feather party" had been keyed to too high a pitch to allow the affair to end in anticlimax. They reacted by expecting that the enemy would seek revenge, perhaps by tarring Mrs. Potter. (Benioff and Bill Smith, because they had interfered with the course of Winchester law, were now classified with the enemy.)

Fred Furniss did want revenge, but through the courts. And because there had been other efforts to return to the lawlessness of the storied West, most of the community agreed that Lillian Potter should be prosecuted.

Bill Campbell was Fred's employer and friend. He drove to the county seat and swore out a complaint. They returned at night and had to pass Skeleton Ranch on their way to Fred's home. The road had been barricaded with logs and old furniture. As the car slowed a voice from the brush shouted, "Halt!"

Campbell swerved his car into the sand and greasewood around the barricade. The bullets just missed his head and pierced the roof of his car. Bill had driven an ambulance in Italy during the war. This situation had a certain element of familiarity. As his car gathered speed he turned and shot back over his shoulder.

Mrs. Potter's homestead lay beyond the Furniss house, well hidden in the mesquite. Here, Jim and Mrs. Potter's sons lay hidden all night, loaded guns and knives in their belts, keeping guard. It had been Al Northey and the deputy who were the outpost on the road. Mrs. Potter's homestead was a poor place for a siege because there was no water. So early in the morning the party moved to Jim Byler's house.

The neighbor boy, on a motorcycle, scouted the road before they moved. Mrs. Potter drove her Packard with Jim, Al, the deputy sheriff and the spotted dog as bodyguards. Her boys drove their jalopy ten feet behind. They passed the Furniss home with rifles and shotguns trained on it.

They stopped at our store. Finding me alone with the children, Mrs. Potter came in with only one gun. She bought supplies. After I had waited on her I walked around the car and as casually as possible I asked Jim if I might have Frank's 45.

"It's loaded," he warned me as he passed it out of the car. "But tell Frank it hasn't been shot." His face was chalky white beneath smudges of dirt, and his hands shook.

Al smiled and raised his hat to me. The deputy watched me with baleful eyes. I realized that I represented the enemy.

For men like Jim, lying alone at night behind creosote bushes, armed and exhausted, it was easy to imagine the gleam of rifles in the brush around him, and the next morning the others readily accepted his story of the night.

The hotel keeper, a woman, on her way to Bill Smith's ranch for milk, was stopped and ordered by the deputy to drive to Banning, to the nearest phone and call to the sheriff in San Bernardino that the party was surrounded and running short of ammunition. Jim had already taken off by an impossible route across dry lake and hills to carry the same message. But he might not get through.

In record time two carloads of deputy sheriffs, the biggest we ever saw, with guns on hips, drove to our store. They got out; of Frank they demanded, "Where is the war?"

"War?" asked Frank. "What are you talking about?" Although we lived less than a mile from Byler's he had been unaware of the siege and only later learned of the message, "Surrounded and running short of ammunition."

"Come on now, don't stall! Where is the war? Men with guns besieged in the greasewood?"

"Oh," said Frank. "If that is what you are looking for you might find it right down the hill."

After they had sorted the facts from the hallucinations the deputies realized the seriousness of the situation. They left two of their number in the district. Later these men told Frank that they had expected murder.

The play went on. Sometimes there would be a signal fire in the mountains south of the oasis, then an answering light from the dry lake. And the caravan would drive past in the night, three cars in formation or with the boys on the running board of their mother's car. But there was less display of guns. When the weather became hot, Mrs. Potter, her family, the local deputy, Jim and Al moved in this fashion to Pipes Canyon, a wooded area between the desert and the mountains. There they camped until time for Lil Potter's trial.

She was finally brought to court on a charge of attempted assault with a deadly weapon. The story had made the Los Angeles papers. Her picture was published with a somewhat flattering account of the affair. The trial was well attended, and Lillian Potter was not a person to resent publicity. She took the witness stand carrying a white rose in her hand.

Her defense stressed the priceless quality of her reputation and made little of the carrying of guns. She stated that she never went into the store without a gun in her hand. No, there was nothing strange about calling on friends at night with guns in hand.

The deputy sheriff, on the stand, could recall nothing but the difficulty he had in holding the dog. He had seen no evil, heard no evil, and certainly would speak no evil. To every question about the events of the night he would reply, "I dunno. I was holding the dog." As to his shots at Bill Campbell's car, that had been in line of duty. Yes, he was armed. "I had a rifle and a Luger. But my star was ashining bright."

Al was eloquent and not inconveniently regardful of the truth. Mercifully, Jim Byler was not put on the stand.

Ben Benioff and Bill Smith were witnesses for the prosecution. They were obviously intelligent, and the defense attorney could not shake their testimony. So he ranted:

"I cannot liken these two men to skunks, to rattlesnakes, or to coyotes. All these have some good quality. I can only call them hyenas.

"I cannot ask you to be swayed by sentiment," he declaimed. "I ask only that you picture this poor widow, alone with her children in a crude frontier community, struggling to provide for them, struggling above all to keep for them a precious heritage, her own unblemished reputation." With tears in his voice he quoted "Mother o' Mine."

He addressed the jury. "Say to this little woman, 'Go back to your desert home, go back to your children, and if any low cur speaks against you, fill him full of lead.' "

The widow was acquitted. But instead of returning to the desert she lived in Banning while things calmed down. It seemed that privately her attorney had given her advice. Jim remained as her guard. He briefly returned to the desert and painted on the roof of his house, "HYENAS — KEEP OUT."

Jim and Bill had been closer friends than men of such different types would have been anywhere else. They had shared their last beans and bacon, and their one set of license plates was used by whichever one had to drive to town. And if one had a clean white shirt, it was loaned for the asking. Jim's sign, a gesture of hate, was not funny.

The local deputy lost his star but he had gained the hand of the lady.

During this time Jim had, I suppose, become sufficiently disaffected to remember that his desert shack had been home and hospitable to two guys who were no worse than skunks, rattlesnakes or coyotes, and definitely better than hyenas.

He returned, came to the store, and we treated him as though he had only casually been away.

He looked for Bill and arranged for him to haul some lumber from the city. They came to the store in the evening and asked me to cash Jim's check so that he could give Bill the money he would need.

Jim, nervous and awkward, wanted to apologize. "It's decent of you to do this for me, Bill," he said. "You wouldn't need to act like this. I done you a lot of dirt."

"Oh heck," said Bill. "You never done me no dirt."

Jim turned to me. "Do you know where I can get some tar?"

Fortunately my face was toward the roll top desk and I leaned low. "No," I replied quite evenly. "We don't carry tar."

"I've got some tar," obliged Bill.

"I'll buy it if you'll let me," said Jim. "I want to paint out that sign on my roof."

"Just take it," said Bill.

Lil also returned, wanting to resume former friendships. She stopped Bill on the road one day as he was pulling up a hill in his Model T truck.

"Bill," she began, "I don't believe in folks treating friends like you do . . ."

Bill stepped on the starter and ground at his gears. Above the roar of the motor he stated clearly, "I don't believe in tarrin' and featherin' my friends either."

Cool Water and the City Hall

Water means life in the desert. The stories of travelers digging with raw fingers in an animal's sump, finding water and struggling on, or not finding water, are legends all too true. Deserted shacks, like prospector's bones, are evidence of hopes that failed. To a community also water means survival.

In Twentynine Palms there was a corps of homesteaders who had come determined to make it home. To some of them, as to Frank, it was a matter of life, to be worth living, or of death, to be preferred. They were not recluses, they were not afraid of hardships or loneliness. They wanted homes on land they owned and a background of sound community life. And so, among their neighbors they "set store" on the man who got his own well. It was possible to live with fair comfort by hauling water, but if a man tried for his own well he was willing to take his chances and he intended to stay.

In the spring we made our decision. We would drill a well.

Twentynine Palms was named for the palm trees clustered around the Oasis of Mara on the south side of the valley. There the water surfaced, and in the earlier years of the century there had been a line of springs along the dike. A large spring had been dug out and covered. It had long been used by travelers, by Indians, and in our day there were still some homesteaders who carried water from it.

Observation shows that there is a fault running northwesterly from east of the oasis to the dry lake. The fault is not plainly marked but it is revealed by clumps of mesquite which is generally supposed to find water for its roots at about thirty feet. To the east of this line wells might be as deep as 300 feet and there were not enough of them to be a reliable guide to the water level. But west of the fault water could be predicted by sighting to an established well and estimating the contour of the land.

We had chosen a homestead in the area of known water levels, but our square half mile of land was on the side of a hill. To minimize cost and risk Frank chose to drill our well on the lower part of the land near to what is now known as Adobe Road.

Before anyone in the desert dug or drilled for water he witched or asked a gifted neighbor to witch for him.

A water witch, or dowser, uses a forked stick, preferably willow, not thicker than a man's little finger. He grasps the forks of the stick in his two hands, thumbs up, and carries it with the stem of the fork pointing upward before him. He walks slowly. The theory is that when an underground stream or water source is crossed the willow rod turns in his hands, bends downward.

The rod will not bend for everyone. There is a psychic factor in the work of the witch. The rod will bend for me, pulling and turning strongly in my hands, so I can speak with experience on one element of the phenomenon. The dowser does not consciously cause the rod to turn.

There was much dispute as to the authority and value of the water witch. But whatever one thought about it, everyone tried dowsing. A well dug or drilled was a major enterprise. A dry well could bankrupt a man financially, or spiritually, when resources were small. The man who dug his own well risked his life. The man who had to have his well drilled could be risking all his savings. Even though he might not have much faith in the water witch he wanted his advice. There remained enough unknown factors.

Granted that the water was there and at a reasonable depth, there were hazards for the man who drilled. The dry sand might cave in. The sand bucket might strike a boulder too large to be moved. The driller might drop a tool and spend all his substance fishing for it. (His cost if he had contracted by the foot. Yours if he worked by the day.)

Even after the casing was down and in water gravel there was still the chance that the perforations might be too coarse and the well would sand up, or that the hole would be so crooked that a rod and pump would not work in it.

Bill Smith contracted to drill our well. He had a homemade well rig, fearfully and wonderfully constructed from odd pieces of machinery and cable. Once when he had to go to town to haul groceries for the store he tossed off at the rig, as he passed, a bundle of pieces of baling wire.

"There," he said to his helper, "is enough repairs to last you a week if I accidently should be gone that long."

On the day that Bill began to drill our well a sea gull came and lit upon our land. It is the only time I ever saw a sea gull in our valley. Frank and I accepted its coming as an omen; we hastened to set out offerings of canned sardines and water. These were disdained, but we were more heartened by the bird than by the water witch.

It was a relaxation and delight to sit for a few minutes and watch the men at work with the drill. As an excuse for my loafing I carried lemonade to the workers. We had no ice; I cooled the lemonade by pouring it into a thin aluminum coffee pot, wrapping that in a wet towel and setting it in the wind for an hour. This offering was never disdained.

The drill had a rhythm like music. There was the pound, pound, pound of the heavy block descending, driving a length of casing into the hole. The sand bucket went down and was hauled up; its jaws opened to empty sand and water. More water must be poured in to lubricate the drill. A new length of casing was fitted into the old and the pile again descended, pound, pound, pound, accompanied by the counter rhythm of the gasoline engine which powered the rig.

When there was a change in the contents of the sand bucket the men would stop to consider it. "Sand again. Sure hope it don't go much deeper."

"Rocks — they could mean trouble. But I reckon we better go on."

"Gravel! Good coarse gravel. Hey, there's water in it! Hey — we got water!"

Frank had not been content with witches and sea gulls. He had borrowed a surveyor's transit and sighted with a carpenter's level to Jim Byler's well which had a known depth to water. Figuring the elevation of the land he had estimated that we would strike water at ninety feet. At ninety-three feet the gravel was wet.

"Ya," said Bill. "But you missed it by three feet."

One burning hot day in June the water poured from our well. It was the most beautiful water I ever saw. Cool, clear water.

This beautiful water, however, was almost half a mile from the site for the tank house. The well had been drilled where the water level was nearest. Now to get good pressure it must be pumped to a tank on the highest part of the land.

In July, the hottest month of the year, Frank had his ditch dug. Most of the work was done by hand so that it gave more employment. It became more of a project than anticipated. Almost as fast as the trench was dug the dry sand refilled it.

Frank had ordered second-hand iron pipe which had been dipped in tar to prevent rust. By the time the pipe was delivered, one quarter mile of trench had been dug and was filling up again.

The men, in order to keep working, offered to take credit for their groceries in the store, instead of cash, for their pay. This seemed like a good idea for about two weeks, but with less paid out for wages more was needed for supplies. The tank house and our house were being built too. It was naturally expected that in the middle of the day there would be a good lunch and cool drinks served in the store. This would be free, of course, since the food came from the shelves and so hadn't cost anything.

It was perhaps fortunate that during this time of problems Frank did not foresee another to come. A year later, when the water system was functioning, the most spectacular water spouts shot up along the pipe line.

Someone would yell into the store, "Hey, your water line is spouting." Frank would leave his work and rush down to plug the pipe. At first it seemed a mystery that the leaks were all on top but it occurred to him that during the days that the pipe lay in the ditch, in the sun, the tar had melted from the top of the pipe, allowing it to rust. He whittled a box of pegs and kept them ready. He would uncover the pipe where it spouted and drive in a peg. The hotter the day, the more leaks. Sometimes the fountain was a welcome shower.

The pipe line was laid and a substantial tank house was built with a big second-hand redwood tank on top. There was a good gasoline engine in place by the well. With a sense of accomplishment and pride Frank started the pump and turned on the water. Then he drove back up the hill.

The water, the beautiful water, was pouring out between the slats of the tank as fast as it came in.

Bill Smith, back from the trip to town for our groceries, watched from the apron of the store. He was tired and he sat, as was his custom on his heels, and watched with sympathy, in silence. He smoked a cigarette and carefully dropped the ashes into the turned-up cuff of his overalls. He considered. This man Frank was from the city. He had been to college and he had been a flyer. He must be smart. He had also worked hard and paid a lot of money to get that water. And now the tank leaked. It was sure too bad.

Mr. Hockett told Frank that all they had to do was to swab the inside of the tank with hot tar. The cracks would fill and the boards would swell.

For a week then, in August, Frank would make a fire, heat a bucket of tar, climb a ladder to the tank carrying the tar, get down into the tank and swab the tar around with a broom. Then he would climb out, down the ladder, get into his car, drive to the well, turn on the water. Hopefully, he would drive back up the hill. And there was the water, the beautiful water, running out the cracks. Again and again, all that week in August, no water ever remained in the tank long enough to swell the boards.

And all that week in August Bill Smith spent part of every day, sitting on his heels, smoking cigarettes, dropping the ashes into his overall cuffs, watching.

In the late afternoon there was shade on the east side of our garage store. One broiling hot day, coming back from the tank to help in the store during the busy hour, Frank stopped for a minute in the shade, and there sat Bill, so relaxed. Frank joined him.

"Bill," he said despairingly, "what would you do if that were your tank?"

Bill took the last puff on his cigarette and carefully dropped the ashes in the cuff of his overalls. "Whatsa matter? Does it leak?"

"It leaks like a sieve."

"Wal, if it was my tank I'd just accidentally throw a handful of raw cement into the water."

"What would that do?"

Bill shook more ashes into his cuff and considered. "Wal," he finally said, "it would stop the leak."

Frank left the shade, climbed up to the tank with a pail of cement and threw in half a shovelful. In less time than it takes to tell the story, the cement, going with the water, percolated into the cracks and the leaking stopped.

We cherished the tradition of the desert that water should be shared. Not everyone observed this. But for almost a year we had hauled water freely from Bill Smith and from Mr. Ed Bixby, now we would share our water.

The tank house was substantial and neat, painted white with a green trim, equipped with a shower head inside and a faucet on the outside. The cold water shower was used by miners and by many homesteaders. The tank was kept full and travelers and neighbors could take water. No one needed to ask.

There was another water station about one hundred feet from the store, five hundred feet north and down slope from the tank house. This one had a hose for filling water barrels. Frank once stopped a man who came day after day with a flat-bed truck covered with barrels.

"Would you mind telling me what you are doing with all that water?"

"Why sure — I'm starting an orchard."

Then there was a lackadaisical chap who stood chatting with me while his water barrel ran over. I finally exploded, "You are welcome to all the water you haul away — but this makes me mad." I must have sounded convincing for he actually ran to turn it off.

The short length of hose used for filling containers disappeared from time to time and had to be replaced. More serious was the theft of a small part from the wellhead which let all the pipe drop. It would have cost about one dollar to buy that part. Frank had to pull up all the pipe from the well in order to replace it. But most people were considerate and some, rather to our surprise, were grateful.

I cannot recall that we had ever felt especially grateful for the water we hauled from our neighbors. It had been part of the desert way of life.

When "Cap" Williamson came to town, his first sermon, preached in the schoolhouse, was entitled "Bagley's Well." But he was new to the ways of the community.

Not long after the tank house was in use someone put up a sign, "City Hall." Everyone laughed and we let it stay. Someone again, we never knew who it was, sent a picture of the tank house with the sign to Ripley of "Believe It Or Not." And this picture with the story that it was the smallest city hall in the world was syndicated all over the United States and much of Europe.

To make it more official a couple chose to be married there. Johnny Kee cut hair there on Saturday. I supposed he moved out if someone wanted a bath. Thus it was a sort of a public building.

And the name of Twentynine Palms, thanks to Mr. Ripley, was in newspapers even before it was on road maps. We had publicity.

"The City Hall." Thanks to Mr. Ripley, the name of Twentynine Palms was in the newspapers even before it was on the maps.

Our boys and a friend in front of the store. The desert cooler in the background. The author, same period, at right.

II. The Community

The School

In the summer of 1927 a committee of homesteaders, including Bill Campbell and Bob McCown drove the long road to San Bernardino, our county seat, to ask the county superintendent of schools, to provide a school for the children of Twentynine Palms. They were very earnest in presenting their request. They were astonished and offended when the superintendent, Miss Ida Collins, a competent woman of middle age, laughed, and the clerks in the office looked up with broad grins.

"My dear people," said the superintendent, "you have had school in Twentynine Palms; you have had two schools. There is none at present. Now you are homesteading and you may seriously believe that you are going to make homes there. You say there are eight children. But most of you are veterans. That means that you can complete your residence in from seven months to two years. In two years or less you will all be gone.

"In desert districts I have seen it happen, not once but many times. The homesteaders come in full of plans and enthusiasm. They must have a school. They want it built by taxpayers' money. Before the year is complete they have moved away.

"Not one dollar of county money for a building will you get from me."

On the way home the road seemed rougher. But the delegation was not discouraged. Their indignation added to their ardor.

The superintendent was legally correct. Under the law school districts by taxation provide their own buildings. In Morongo district, which is as large as some states, there had been through the years a number of schools in cabins, but with teachers paid for by the county. One of these had been closed when it was discovered that the teacher had only one pupil to instruct. There had been eight, but the others had moved away. Another teacher had fled because an irate parent had come to her tent, pulled it down around her head, and threatened to "fill her full of lead."

The Twentynine Palms schoolhouse, so the committee determined, would be a worthy and permanent building. There was no tax money available in our frontier of desert and desert mountains. Then the homesteaders would build it themselves.

I have wondered sometimes if the superintendent had not laughed would they have waited until Twentynine Palms was a recognizable town? And if they had waited would there ever have been a town?

For there were not many settlers, and no center could be called a village. Only four or five families had children, and these were poorest of all. Some of those most enthusiastic in their demand for a school had neither children, nor money, nor strength to give to the building. The things the superintendent had said were true of most settlements in the desert.

The Campbells gave five acres at the corner of their homestead for a site. Three hundred dollars was raised for materials. Most of this was a gift of two or three but many contributed. It seems a ridiculously small amount today, but for a scattered community of homesteaders in the desert it was a large sum then. There were more who were generous with time. One old man said, "I've no money, but I'm just full of day's work."

And so they built, arguing democratically all the while as to whether they were building in the wrong place and whether the building was not, after all, too large. It was twenty by twenty-eight. It was planned that the room would accommodate twenty pupils and there were only eight in the territory to be served. Only a few homesteaders had houses as large as the schoolroom.

But they built substantially and well. By way of adorn-

School built by homesteaders in 1927, "They built substantially and well."

The old school was enlarged and the new room so arranged that it might serve as community hall. The wide porch could serve as a stage with the audience seated on the ground.

ment they added a bell tower, and they painted it glistening white trimmed with green. And it did not belong to the county! The homesteaders built it. The school was their own.

Their pride and possessiveness were justified. But because of it they became a headache to teachers, school board, and county.

As a community we were of many kinds and many minds. Most were public spirited, energetic and generous. But we did not work in peace and harmony. One old woman coined a word that suited us well. "There is too much discontention here," she said.

Sincerity, interest, enthusiasm, these we had in common. Inevitably we disagreed. It used to be said that we should have more brotherly love. Frank had grown up with five brothers. It seemed to him that brotherly love was just about what we did have.

The state law required that the superintendent of schools should furnish a teacher when there were six children without a school within reasonable distance. The school nearest to Twentynine Palms was in the Pipes, a desert mountain country forty miles north and west. In November school was opened in the little white schoolhouse. Our John made the ninth pupil and the teacher sent to us brought two of her own.

She was middle-aged and unhappy over almost everything. She was so uninventive that she complained of a lack of counters for the first grade, this in a country that had more beans and pebbles than anything else.

The people who had given and worked so proudly for the building of the school were outraged that the teacher did not also love and cherish it. A group met by chance one day in our store. The teacher happened to come in. Betty Campbell said:

"Now while we are together let's sit right down here and talk about this school. *I* couldn't live in a room with finger smudges on the doors."

For two hours they talked there in our grocery-nursery-kitchen while potential customers apologetically sidled out in order not to interfere, and my hungry children were bribed with cookies to be quiet and forget lunch.

Finally the teacher won the sympathy of most of the group just because she was so out-talked and overwhelmed with criticism. She repeated over and over her defense. "I was not hired to be janitor." And so the indignation meeting organized itself into a committee, visited the school that weekend and personally scrubbed floors, washed windows and white woodwork.

They left the building shining and attractive in its bare cleanliness. The next week the teacher and her two children moved in. She had been living in a cabin half a mile away and she was afraid of the range cattle she sometimes passed on her way to school.

There had been a Morongo School District since about 1920. Undoubtedly it took its name because the first school was near Morongo, thirty miles west of Twentynine Palms. De Foss Geil had been clerk of the board since 1923. In 1927 there was a small school in the Pipes and Mrs. Camilla Hudson was trustee. These excellent people seem to have been ignored by the homesteaders in Twentynine Palms. But school boards have three members and I was appointed to fill the vacancy.

I recall vividly the day I was notified of the honor about to be bestowed. I was doing the family wash in a tin tub set up on boxes in front of the store when Bob McCown, a former salesman and book agent with a silver tongue, presented himself as a committee of one. The county superintendent had agreed to appoint a trustee, formally chosen by the community, to the district board. I had been selected and was being honored, said Mac, because I had so much patience. Rashly he added, "You will need it."

Mac's diplomacy was for once in error. As I have mentioned on nearly every page, I had three small boys and I had often been accused, and suspected myself, of having too much patience. It troubled me that I should be chosen as school trustee because of a quality of such dubious advantage.

My choice of the apron or porch in front of the store as a place for washing things may seem eccentric but it was there that our water barrels stood. I could draw water from the spigots at the bottom and so in that place I had running water. It was an arrangement much envied by homesteaders who hauled their water in cans. Also, there was, alas, no steady stream of customers at the store. We could expect, at certain hours, privacy.

And that is how it happened that when the county superintendent, Miss Collins, called to meet me for the first time, I was washing my hair in front of the store. She was obviously not impressed with me or my qualifications. I doubt whether even my notorious patience would have appealed to her.

Miss Collins was capable and conscientious, but she did not like the desert. The law required her to visit every school in the county once a year. The trips were long, the roads rough and dusty, the weather usually either too hot or too cold. She was never prejudiced in our favor by the time she arrived.

Moreover our very civic virtues, our pride and possessiveness, our enthusiastic and often unreasonable demands for our school, made us a nuisance. Already we had begun writing petitions. Gradually they became our favorite indoor sport and amounted to an addiction.

Under state law our school had the status of an emergency school. The school in Pipes Canyon was the regular school of the district. This meant only that the District of Morongo, with its many square miles and few inhabitants, could pay its share of expenses for only one school. The Pipes school was already established, and the Twentynine Palms' school must therefore have its teacher furnished and its expenses paid from an "emergency fund" controlled by the superintendent.

When it was rumored that our beautiful new institution

of learning, with eleven pupils, was inferior to a school in the Pipes, community pride was offended.

One of the most enthusiastic supporters of our school was Ed Duquette. He was a veteran, a bachelor, and because he had tuberculosis, he avoided children. Undersized, he had a compensating quality of combativeness. He came to me burning with indignation because he had heard that the school in the Pipes was better equipped than ours. As trustee, what was I going to do about it?

A visit to the rival institution was in order. Ed acted as my chauffeur and we drove to the Pipes. The edifice we found was a modern version of a pioneer cabin, built of materials on hand. In this case, tin cans! Some homesteader had made forms for his walls, filled them with tin cans, and poured in cement. The floor was thinly coated with cement which had broken off in patches. In this structure the school was housed. Sanitary arrangements were one outhouse and one tin basin for washing up. The maps, the desks, were all more worn and shabby than ours.

We called on Mrs. Hudson, the trustee, who lived near by. She was a woman of culture, a former teacher; her husband was a lawyer who had to live in the desert because of his health. Her own children were in the school; she was personally doing all she could to supplement the inadequate instruction. Obviously, she thought the people in Twentynine Palms were brash and unreasonably demanding. We, too, should adapt ourselves to circumstances.

Ed Duquette and I drove home humbled by the recollection of our burning jealousy but not reconciled to passivity. We were glad that Twentynine Palms had a neat schoolhouse painted white, and two outhouses, and two tin wash basins on the back stoop.

A few weeks later Ed, who had been a plumber when able to work, personally raised three hundred dollars from friends outside the valley, and constructed from galvanized steel pipe, bars, swings and trapezes; play equipment worthy of any schoolyard.

But the teacher's discontent and that of the community

culminated in her resignation. The school closed, pending the coming of a new teacher. This time, surely, we would be sent one young, competent and personable. Literally and figuratively, we hoped for no more smudges on the walls.

A message from the county office struck us with dismay and confusion. No teacher would be appointed to Twentynine Palms for the balance of the year. (It was then March.) The reasons, enough in an office polished and orderly; our attendance record was not good, our community was not a fit place to send a young teacher.

Earlier in the year there had occurred the incident known to fame and the *Los Angeles Examiner* as the "Twentynine Palms Tar and Feather Pary." The trial of the widow who had led the party had taken place in the courthouse of San Bernardino. It was a bonanza for feature writers who saw only the humor and the combined picturesqueness of the old South and the wild West in the situation. Miss Collins, whose office was only one floor removed from the court, frequently attended, but she was not looking for humor.

She heard the defense that in Twentynine Palms everyone carried a gun. She had listened to Al Northey and the deputy on the stand. She did not consider that had we really been a horse opera country the matter would have been settled quite differently and the County Court House would not have been amazed and amused. It was the determination of the majority to have a decent community that had forced to public attention the group who wanted to live by other codes.

The widow with her white rose had been acquitted, but the village had won a victory of sorts. She had moved away. The teacher who bewailed her lot had left us. The schoolhouse could now be all that a little white school should be.

But it was an emergency school and under the law we were dependent for a teacher on the county superintendent. And Miss Collins said that Twentynine Palms did not deserve another teacher.

Betty Campbell, who had always attended private school, made an offer which was generous and which to her seemed entirely reasonable. She would pay the salary of a teacher. Only desirable children would attend. The school and its premises would be above reproach. I think she never quite understood why her offer was refused.

In this crisis it was Bob McCown, the salesman, who came to the rescue. He was perhaps the sickest man in town but he had his gift. He drove the long road to San Bernardino, called on Miss Collins, and she sent us another teacher.

The new teacher was a maiden and a lady. With cool and capable hands she gathered up the loose reins of discipline. In the remaining two months the children learned enough to prepare them for the next grades.

The teacher chose to live in a small grey cabin on our homestead and so I came to know her slightly. Before she left she told me that she had been warned not to associate with the people of the community, who were low rough characters. When the school term was completed and she came to say goodby, she added quietly, "I am sorry not to have known you better."

Those two months with a school which was peaceful and well conducted had restored our pride and confidence. During the summer Bill Campbell gave fencing enough to enclose an acre for playground. The men of the district put up the fence in a solid, workmanlike way. Money was raised for a well, even the children contributed. Rent was paid for the well rig but most of the labor was donated. Again, men who had no children worked long and faithfully. A windmill was erected and a tank stand built.

A windmill in the desert is a beautiful thing! In the silence and oppressive heat at noon, or under the stars at night, the whir of the blades, even the squeak of the rod pumping, are like music. They sing of cool water, water to drink, water that flows, green trees growing. Trees grew up around the tank stand, birds nested there, and the children played in the water that trickled away, content in the midst of a land of shimmering heat.

For as soon as the well was completed, Jim Byler, of the quivery hands, who said, "I don't like kids," went to town and brought back a truckload of trees for the school grounds.

"Nurseryman I know gave them to me," he said. "I told him I wanted a donation for a veteran's cemetery." Jim was pleased with himself for having obtained them in that way. Had he simply told the truth, that he wanted the trees for a desert school, there would have been no art in his achievement.

He had brought Chinese elm, locusts, umbrella trees and Carolina poplars. After planting them we also set out switches of athol trees. Each school child was assigned a tree to care for that year.

The school began its second year proudly equipped. There was an acre of schoolyard neatly fenced, a building with a belltower and a bell to ring, swings and bars for play time, a well and windmill, green trees growing. And it belonged to us, to the people of the frontier known as Twentynine Palms. Not a dollar of county money had been spent on it. In fact, because it did not belong to the school district, not one dollar of public money could be spent on it, and money was needed for upkeep.

Hunting through the school law I found the answer to that problem. The district could legally pay rent for a building used to house a school. So another town meeting was called in the schoolhouse. Everyone came and voted.

Mrs. Campbell deeded the land on which the school was built to a "Holding Committee" elected by the meeting. This committee received rent from the district board and used the money for maintenance and improvement. The community had invested about twenty-five hundred dollars in the school and grounds; the board paid thirty dollars a month rent, and it was still our own!

The teacher sent to us for the second year was a cheerful and competent young woman. She lived in our small gray cabin, known for years as "the teacher's cabin," and in spite of being warned against us, she made friends all through the community.

During that year the children in the Pipes moved away and that school was closed. Twentynine Palms school became the "permanent school" in the Morongo district. Thereafter the teacher was hired by the trustees.

The teacher we employed was young and pretty, with a soft voice, appealingly feminine. She had just graduated from UCLA. She found her way out to apply for the school in the midst of a torrential August rain which washed out roads. She was undaunted. The children loved her.

I was making an official visit to the school one day that autumn when Bill Smith, acting as interested citizen, also came to visit. After half an hour he whispered to me to inquire whether school was in session or whether it was recess. That a bachelor like Bill visited school was, of course, significant.

For the first time we found it necessary to stock shoe polish in our store.

I, too, wanted to make a good impression on this gentle young teacher Elvira, not for myself but for the community which had such a dubious reputation in the county.

Mrs. Campbell, who had been generous to the school in many ways, lived in a house which, though small and home-built, expressed her background of travel and culture. I asked her if I might bring the new teacher for tea. After that arrangement had been made I remembered that ladies wore hats to tea. A hat — what was it? Surely in some remote past I had owned one.

After some search I found a nondescript beige felt at the back of the wardrobe. It was the casual type which survives changing styles and which no one looks at anyway. But it had been kicking around in that wardrobe for several years and it was far too dirty to go to tea. Hopefully, I drew some gasoline from the service station pump and scrubbed that hat with a nail brush. It looked quite decent.

I dusted the car, not too much, and drove Elvira to tea.

Mrs. Campbell was charming. Her homestead house with its adobe fireplace, an oriental rug making a pool of glowing color on the cement floor, a gleaming silver tea service, was all that I had hoped. Although the day was warm, there was a fire of desert driftwood on the hearth, and Mrs. Campbell left the door open into her bright garden.

But the odor of gasoline began to fill the room, overpowering the fragrance of flowers, of jasmine tea. Mrs. Campbell began to fidget. She rose and looked impatiently out toward her garage-workshop. At last she said:

"I am so sorry, but I don't know what I can do about this dreadful odor of gasoline. Someone must have spilled it about the garage."

I snatched off my hat and flung it through the open door. "No," I said, "It's that!"

In the late spring the board invited Elvira to return for another year, but she refused and told me shyly that she had decided which man she would marry.

Alnora Earenfight, who had come to the desert for her health and who the year before had also decided which one she would marry, was elected to the school board that June. Her early teaching experience had given her a viewpoint more practical than my own. Together we hired a young married woman who had taught for several years. She was not gentle, but she was an excellent room manager. The school needed her firm hand. There were thirty-eight children in one room, requiring instruction of eight grades.

Financially our district, which was growing rapidly, was always hampered by low assessed valuation and by the fact that state funds were always based on the attendance of the previous year. An added drain was a transportation allowance made by the trustees to the parents of children who lived more than two miles from school. The rate paid was small, but where several families combined to use a car, the allowance paid for the gasoline.

This led to another set of problems. On one route a girl of twelve drove ten miles to school gathering children as she came, until the last to get on hung on from the running boards. We needed a school bus desperately, but we had no funds to provide one. The laws of California, excellent in their intent, set the standards of safety for transportation so high that it was impossible for a poor district to buy a bus.

When one day an officer in a high-powered car drove the one hundred miles from San Bernardino to inspect our bus, Alnora and I were furious. Furious, because although we squeezed every dollar, we were too poor to have a bus, and that trip must have cost the county at least thirty of those beautiful round unsqueezed dollars. A phone call from the first floor to the third floor of the courthouse would have saved the trip.

Our indignation gave us new resolution. The following year, thanks to the homely ingenuity of Bill Smith, our school had a bus. It met all the legal requirements, but certainly no legislator had imagined such a vehicle. There must be safety glass; there was safety glass in the only place there was any glass, the windshield. There were correct brakes, an emergency exit in the rear, signaling devices, even a fog light. (Our desert never has fog.) Our bus passed inspection. But what the astonished eyes of the officer saw was an old truck chassis, fitted with wooden sides with a slit for ventilation and viewing the landscape, and with wooden benches running front to rear. The like had never been seen before, but it was infinitely safer than a jalopy driven by a twelve year old.

Miss Collins came out to see our vehicle and for the first time she seemed to be impressed. The next year she assisted the district with emergency funds and we were able to afford a secondhand bus of more conventional type.

Three R's in Two Rooms

The one room was so crowded in the spring of 1931 that the teacher could barely walk between the seats. It was necessary to plan another room and provide a second teacher. The "holding committee" deeded the school property to the Morongo District so that a bond could be voted. The bonds were to be in the amount of five thousand dollars. It now seems an absurdly small sum, but it was then close to the legal limit of indebtedness for the district.

An opposition party appeared; the lady of tar and feather party fame drove around the valley with banners on her truck, "School Bonds — NO." In spite of this pageantry and much effort at personal persuasion the bond issue was approved by a wide margin. But more trouble came; the amount of the bonds was so small that the usual buyers were not interested. The county treasurer was authorized to buy such issues, but the officials scanning the records found a technical flaw in the oath of the election board in the western half of the district.

Summer was passing — it would soon be time for school to open. The school board paid out of its own pockets for the services of a lawyer to get a decision validating the bonds. A contractor finally broke ground on the day school opened.

Most fortunately there had been a telephone linesmen camp at Smith's ranch during the previous year and there were available two large screened dormitory rooms. And again, fortunately, the weather remained mild for two months. Until the new rooms of the schoolhouse were ready, classes were held in the dormitories of the abandoned linesmen's camp.

That was the first year that the Twentynine Palms

School had two teachers. They were both just out of college and both excellent. Before school opened I helped them unpack and check the texts and supplies. I was thoroughly able and accustomed to such work; one of the girls looked so fragile that we had hesitated about employing her. They were both not only deferential and courteous, they were solicitous. "Let us," they would say if a box was heavy. If they saw me about to stoop to pick up a book they would both stoop so quickly that we very nearly bumped our heads together. I was shocked into consciousness that my thirty-five years seemed an advanced age. It was confusing.

The slender girl who had appeared so fragile not only taught thirty children in four upper grades that year but found time and energy to be athletic coach for the big boys. She proved to be such a good pitcher that the men of the community were inspired to form teams and sand-lot ball was played.

For the first game the teacher pitched and the umpire, Ed Malone, brandished an empty Luger as he called the strikes and balls. The game soon settled into serious competition and has been enjoyed in our town ever since. It is still fun for old-timers to remember Bill Hockett running bases with a pipe in his mouth, and the sad glad days when the sons began replacing their fathers in the pitcher's box.

If we had employed an architect for our new building his fee would have required much of that bond issue. Les Earenfight, an engineer and draftsman, drew our plans. The old room was enlarged and the new room, designed for primary grades, was arranged so that it might also serve as community hall. The wide porch which gave shade for lunch hour and recitation groups could also serve as stage for graduation exercises in June when the audience could be seated on the grounds. The primary room had low, movable tables, a piano, and a smooth maple floor. On Saturday nights it became a dance hall; on Sundays, the meeting place for a church group.

The Parent Teacher Club and the Legion Auxiliary took

turns in sponsoring dances. Young and old came; fathers gravely waltzed with tiny daughters, mothers tried to learn to follow, not to lead, when they danced with their sons. The music might be only Bill Barnett at the piano but he had rhythm, and he made up for the lack of drums by beating steadily with his left foot. Later my Johnny, with a guitar and a larger foot, supported him. And still later, Les Cross, a carpenter with a musical saw, carried the melodies.

We were not critical of our musicians. Sometimes they were paid, sometimes not, but they played for the fun of it and we danced for the fun of it.

Our constable, Jack Cones, was always present in his official capacity. A county ordinance required that but it would have taken an act of Congress to keep him away. He weighed two hundred and fifty pounds, and he suffered from an old war injury in his foot, but he never sat out a number. He might grumble all the next week about how his feet hurt, but by eight o'clock on Saturday he had always recuperated. To dance with him on a crowded floor was quite an experience. Of course people do not intentionally bump constables, but I have been his partner when a gyrating jitterbug flung himself full tilt into Jack's back. Across his broad shoulder I could see the collision but never feel a tremor.

The younger miners from the hills came in to dance and often brought their bottles with them. They never drank inside the school; the state law forbidding smoking and drinking on school premises was ostensibly respected, but they retreated to their cars between numbers. Sometimes the sponsoring committees regarded this practice with favor. There was no admission charge for the dances. Times were hard for this was in the early depression years, and it was considered that the man who could not afford to pay a quarter for an evening of fun probably needed it most of all. But the sponsoring organization was always trying to raise money for some worthy project, and the miners earning from four to six dollars a day were our monied class. Late in the evening, but not too late, a hat was passed, and a mining man slightly inebriated was likely to be more generous than one cold sober. He might even put in a dollar!

The trustees had a certain responsibility for the conduct of the parties. It required a nice balance to keep the affairs wholesome enough for the very young, approved by the staid and middle-aged, and lively enough for husky young miners with no place else to go.

If Jack Cones were requested to take a man off the floor because he was bleary-eyed or unsteady on his feet, he managed it so that no one was embarrassed. If it was a winter night he walked the fellow outside to clear his head and then let him come back in and watch from the wall. "A guy too drunk to dance is too drunk to drive home," he explained. And long hair though I was, I never saw a rowdy crowd, or a bottle inside the room, or heard profanity.

In matters of dress, too, we had a great tolerance for one another. Two things were not socially permissible, dirt or ostentation. We were somewhat resentful of a young buck with a fine torso who used to arrive in his white cotton undershirt on very warm nights. "Here I am, you lucky people," he would shout. And after every orchestra number he would clap and call to the crowd, "What's the matter, don't you like it?" But it was really more fun when he was there, and no one ever went so far as to ask him to wear a shirt. He might have felt unwelcome.

At the other extreme was Louie Jacobs, an elderly man who was equally a patron of the beer parlor and the Parent Teacher Club. He often wore a tuxedo and gold bedroom slippers. But most of the men wore their best sport shirts, seldom coats or ties, and the women wore pretty "casual" dresses.

After the grammar school graduation in June the audience remained to congratulate and to dance with the graduates. The little girls in their first long "formals" with ribbons in their hair, their wide eyes shining, looked like desert wildflowers. For that occasion we all wore our best. To a little girl in her first formal even a schoolroom dance can seem a princess' ball, and shining eyes can create a spell of glamor which even the weary and the sophisticated can feel.

The dances closed at midnight out of respect for the Sabbath. Sunday morning the schoolhouse functioned again as a place of worship. Sunday school opened at ten, and it was to be hoped that the floor had been swept and all the bottles around the fence disposed of in the interval.

It was years before there was an organized church in Twentynine Palms, but soon after we had a school building there was a Sunday school. It was conducted by the Reverend William Carle and his wife, May, who had been missionaries in Alaska. Like everything else it was home-spun and informal. Teachers must be selected on the basis of willingness rather than training. This encourages enthusiasm and devotion, but sometimes unusual theories were expounded.

However, the most impressive Easter pageant I ever watched was staged in our school. It was imaginative, reverent, beautiful. On the way home one of my little boys, Alan, spoke after a long silence. He said:

"I can see what you mean about the Sunday radio comedians."

A memorable funeral was solemnized in the one-room school in Yucca Valley. A ten-year-old boy had died in his remote desert home. His father, Walter Kerr, was one of the school board. He wanted his son to be buried from the schoolhouse. His playmates could be there, and the neighbors.

The room was full; we sat two in a seat. The small coffin rested on a primary table at the front. It was banked with grey-green branches of juniper. There were no flowers. It was still early for wildflowers. Two spots of color stood out brightly. A cowboy pallbearer wore a red neckerchief. It was his best. The school flag hung on the wall near the door.

The boy's mother had asked if her son's coffin might be

draped with a flag. She was an army wife and the symbol would have comforted her. But the father, an old regular army sergeant, told her that honor must be reserved for those who had served. A neighbor, chosen because he was a good man, read from the Bible; a quartet sang softly. And while they sang some breeze from an opened door caught the schoolroom flag, blew it gently, draped it gracefully across the coffin. The man who had read reached to take it up but the old sergeant raised his hand. They let it lie as it had fallen.

After there were two teachers in the Twentynine Palms school a year of high school subjects was added, taught by the teacher of the four advanced elementary grades. A provision of the school code, allowing for junior high schools, could be interpreted to make this possible. The provision of one year of high school work was inadequate, but it was a beginning. Our enrollment was too small, our assessed valuation too low, to permit us to form a high school district. But we remained a large district in area and in ideas.

Under the code the school received more money for a high school pupil than for one in grammar school. After two years of scheming and penny-pinching the board approached the county superintendent with a new idea. We saw our way clear to hire another teacher, rent a room in a cottage, give two years of high school work. Miss Collins was skeptical but she was getting used to us. "Go ahead, " she said. "But don't come to me for money."

We could allow ten dollars a month for janitor's services, twenty-five dollars a month for rent, and just $1200 a year for teacher's salary. But these were depression years, our applicants came to us.

Walter Ketcham was then the second local member of the school board. He sent me a note, "I like this man. Hire him if you agree with me."

The man sat on my couch, his long legs stretched out in front. His wife, slender with black eyes, wearing a red tam, sat beside him. I had seen the applicant's papers. He had no experience, but the president of Occidental College had written, "one of the finest minds I have encountered in ten years of teaching."

But my ideas and those of the community were large. We would expect him to teach, beside all the required subjects for two grades, physical education, manual training, and music.

"Can you teach music?"

"Not qualified," said Theodore M. Hayes.

Mary, his wife broke in, "Oh, but Ted has a very good baritone voice. I know because I teach music now, — and I could help."

"You are teaching? What are you paid?"

"Oh, a little more than you can offer. But that does not matter. If Ted comes, I'll come too."

And so they came. In that two years of high school were provided the basic subjects, manual training, with the shop on a screen porch of the cottage, music, and sewing for the girls. For this last, Alnora Earenfight gave her time. She had taught it professionally in another state. While the boys had shop, Mary took the girls in her car to Alnora's house. The girls could not be given credit for this course, but they learned to sew.

Ted was physical education director. The boys played football in the wide road which ran past the swimming pool. He broke his glasses twice and his ribs once — or was it the other way around?

There had now been provided as many years of high school work as were possible in a grammar school district under the school code. It seemed a good idea to change the code.

The trustees drew up an amendment to the school law to apply to small districts, and submitted it to the county office. It was reasonable and possible, the legal advisor reported. But how, we asked ourselves, would we get it on the floor of a busy legislature?

Mr. Burton Thrall had recently been elected to the office of county superintendent of schools, replacing Miss

Above: Cottage and cabin on the Legion grounds were used for high school.

Ted and Mary Hayes lived in another cottage, near by. Their back house came complete with black widow spiders. "The young have good hearts. They thought it was funny."

Collins. He came to see our school. He listened with respect to the account of our stringent financing, our ambitions. He did not laugh at the idea of amending the state law; he studied our problem.

It was possible for our district to join a union high school district. Morongo was contiguous to three, although remote from all the high schools and center of administration. Mr. Thrall advised us to join Victorville, which was conversant with desert areas, and not too afraid of acquiring a poor relation.

This happened in August. Thus ended the responsibility of the Morongo District for its swan child. And it ended also our contract with our high school teacher, Ted Hayes.

Mr. Ketcham was secretary of the board. It was his lot to break the news. Ted and Mary were away on vacation; it was the end of summer, they had saved just enough money to get them back to Twentynine Palms. The official letter when it reached them tactfully broke the news all over the first of two typewritten pages.

"We can no longer offer employment. The hiring of the high school teacher is not within our province. The association has been most pleasant and satisfactory. The Morongo Elementary Board regrets . . ."

Ted was reading aloud to Mary. They were stunned. It was September, too late for another teaching position; they had twenty dollars in the bank.

At the very end of the second typewritten page, — "The Victorville High School Board have engaged another teacher, a young lady who is highly recommended. They wish to retain you as principal at a salary of $1800."

The young have good hearts. They thought it was funny!

A Long Way to Go

When the homesteaders were coming to Twentynine Palms during the twenties they were using the road which had been worn and rutted by the horse-drawn vehicles freighting to Dale and the other mining camps years before. It was single track, winding to dodge boulders, Joshua trees and even greasewood bushes. A car traveling at more than fifteen miles an hour might tip over. If two cars met one had to pull off. It was then common courtesy for the other driver to wait and be sure that the car which had left the road could get back on again.

The road went close to Warren's Well, a watering place, and then on twenty-four miles to the Oasis of Mara at Twentynine Palms.

In the area of Twentynine Palms there was a secondary road, little more than a trail, coming from Mesquite Springs, meandering across the quarter section which we homesteaded and over the hill to the Oasis and the Gold Park Hotel. From there other roads had been worn by miners and settlers south into Gold Park and north along the section line that is now called Utah Trail, then east toward Amboy.

The most urgent needs of the homesteaders were for a school and for roads. It is to their credit that the first endeavor had been for a school. This was given priority even though only four families had children, whereas everyone needed a road.

They organized their efforts through town meetings. There was no store, no post office, and no phone. The call to a meeting must have been carried by men driving across the sand from house to house.

To be eligible to vote in a town meeting a person must

live near enough and be concerned enough to get there.
They met at night on the grounds of the Gold Park Hotel
and drew their cars in a circle. People sat on running
boards or on seat cushions taken from their cars. There was
a table for the chairman and a gasoline lantern for light.

Thus the first organization in the community was
formed, the Twentynine Palms Road Improvement Association. A treasurer and a chairman, Bill Campbell, were
elected. Discussion began.

Where should the road be built? Why did not San Bernardino County build it?

These two questions were related. The county had good
reason to spend no money building a road for a handful of
voters who paid almost no taxes and could not agree on
where they wanted a road.

The first survey through the area had been made in
1855 by Colonel Washington. He had surveyed the San
Bernardino Base Line. The old wagon road to the mines
kept as close to it as the mountains allowed. Some people
wanted this crooked rutted road kept and improved. Others
demanded that a new road be graded one mile north of the
base line. More people were living two or three miles north
and wanted the new route graded on a line two miles north
of the base line.

When self interest was involved discussion flared into
angry argument. At a second or third meeting it was voted
to appoint a qualified man to roughly survey the one mile
and two mile section lines running west from Utah Trail
and advise which would be more feasible. By this time it
had been made clear that the county would not help. The
men of the community had determined to build for themselves.

The man appointed to report on the routes was Ben
Benioff. He had a degree in engineering. For him it was a
challenge to do work for which he had been trained. He
made a trip to the city and returned with a license as surveyor.

He reported on the One Mile route that the first six

miles would require crossing a hill and then a long stretch of sandy wash, this through the district now called "Smoke Tree." Anyone familiar with the desert knows that smoke trees grow in sandy washes which are subject to floods. To construct a firm straight road on that line would require more money than the community could manage.

The two mile line offered no special problems. It could be made passable with such labor and equipment as was available. After six miles this road could be joined to the one mile section line and some parts of the old wagon road could be straightened and used.

It was voted to accept the report made by Benioff, but argument did not end. No one actually lived on the Two Mile line at that time (summer of 1927). Most settlers lived in the shallow water area near Mesquite Springs. The Donnells, Hassell and Norman, had built a substantial house on the One Mile line.

Again discussion led to shouting. Finally someone said, "Let's get to work. Everyone who will work meet on Utah Trail by the school house. Bring your picks and shovels and let's go." The meeting was adjourned.

And so work began on the Two Mile Road. It was hot. Many of the men were veterans with asthma or tuberculosis who should not have worked at all, but they did what they could. The women met with Betty Campbell and prepared lunches. At noon they piled the food on a pickup truck, drove to where the men were working and served from the tail-gate. In deference to the ladies the men put on their shirts and washed from water bags of drinking water. Coffee was reheated in the ashes left from burning greasewood and roots.

They were only a handful of men and they needed forty miles of road. To heck with the county!

Bill Campbell lent a secondhand tractor and a scraper. A plow and chains for pulling were also loaned. A man who had asthma too seriously to allow him to work paid for the gasoline. A heavy drag was built of scraps of wood and iron. When they had cleared rocks and brush from a mile of road they dragged it and men rested on their shovels to admire and exult.

Ben Benioff, with his transit, tried to keep ahead of the work crew. He knew how it should be done. "Hold it a day or two," he implored. "I need to tie it to the base line every mile."

Tie it to the base line? Wait while Ben chained six miles north and south and six miles east and west to check the line of the road? With all the empty desert sand and so far to go? What difference would a few feet make?

(Fifteen years later Colonel Benioff was in charge of construction on the Ledo-Burma road across the mountains between India and China. He must have laughed then, remembering his experience in road building in Twentynine Palms.)

The few but determined men who still wanted the One Mile Road made trips to the board of supervisors, trying to get their backing. This made the supervisors certain that we did not know what we wanted. These men, led by Hassell Donnell and encouraged by Lida, went to work on their own. The women helped with lunches and Lida's apple pies at noon. They also threw rocks off the road and piled brush for burning. Some men worked on both roads to show their good will.

Within a few months there were two passable roads which joined six miles west of Utah Trail where the Lear Road now joins the Twentynine Palms Highway. The work continued until there was thirty miles of road dragged and wide enough for two cars to pass. Other communities joined the effort and straightened and smoothed their trail. About two years later the county took over maintenance, but it was not until W.P.A. labor was available that the road was paved. The county adopted the One Mile Road as the Twentynine Palms Highway because it could continue directly to the mining area and to the Colorado River.

In the meantime, "back at the ranches" nearly every homesteader was trying to improve his own road. After a rain they were out with drags, smoothing their trails. Children joyfully rode on the drags to give them weight. The greasewood smell so sweet after a rain. It was like a holiday.

Everyone talked and argued roads. (And yet, our great delight had been to drive where there were none.) People who had been for the One Mile Road might not speak to those who wanted the Two Mile Road. There was a division of feeling long continued as "North Side-South Side."

The homesteaders still had a long way to go and a rough road to travel. Not everyone had worked and they had not agreed, but they had accomplished. There was a new sense of pride and confidence.

The Campbells

The story of Betty and Bill Campbell is a story of love and will. Elizabeth W. Crozer had been born into a family of great wealth. The Pennsylvania farm of which she writes in her book "The Desert Was Home" was an estate with a staff of gardeners, grooms, stewards and many servants. She was brought up, however, strictly and simply. Her father was an autocrat, strong of will.

Betty adored him, but she had inherited his will. Once she rode a horse which was forbidden to her; she was thrown and hurt. Her father gathered her in his arms to carry her to the house. On the way he said:

"A girl who was born to be hanged can't die any other way."

She told me this story many times, and always there was an inflection of tenderness and pride.

She tells that Bill and she had met at the war-time wedding of a friend and had fallen deeply in love. They had yielded to her parent's opposition to war-time marriages. Bill went overseas in 1918. He served as an ambulance driver in Italy, was decorated for bravery, was burned by mustard gas, captured and held prisoner. For months Betty did not know whether he lived. When, after the armistice, she heard that he was coming home, she flung herself into her father's arms for comfort in the flood of her emotion.

Her parents wanted her to marry a suitor who was her equal in social position and in family power and wealth. Nevertheless, when she was firm in her determination to marry Bill, they gave her a wedding with family and close friends, followed by a reception for one thousand guests.

Betty and Bill were joyful and full of hope.

Bill was Western. Orphaned while young he had made

his way living much of his life in the out of doors. He was of Scottish ancestry, calm and stable. Betty said, "Perhaps our only similarity is that we are both fair and blue-eyed."

She never talked of the break with her family. Bill once told Frank that he had refused to work for her father. He could not accept a position as a junior, doubtfully tolerated, in a wealthy, autocratic empire. This is easy to understand. Betty's first loyalty was to her husband. The clash of wills between father and daughter is hard to imagine. He disinherited her.

They moved to the West, lived for a year or two in Pasadena. Bill had been burned with mustard gas shortly before the war's end. The condition of his lungs was serious and Southern California gave him little relief. He was struggling to make a living during a period when Betty twice lost premature babies. She would not appeal to relatives for help they needed because she feared that this humiliation might utterly crush and destroy her husband.

It was Dr. Luckie who advised them to try the desert climate. He warned Betty that Bill should use his throat as little as possible. He did not want to alarm Bill by stressing this; he told Betty to avoid conversation with him. During those first hard months when they camped at the Oasis of Mara, living where wild burros broke into their tent and nibbled their food, she was constantly aware of that warning, not to engage her husband in conversation.

One of their routine tasks was to go to the mesquite near the dry lake, about five miles north of the Oasis, to gather firewood. In the sand they found flint chippings and arrow points. When they showed these to Bill McHaney, the old prospector who visited their camp, he told them about the Indians who had lived in the hill country, south of them, who migrated leaving their cooking pots and ollas hidden in the crevices and caves of boulders.

Betty realized that they were in a virgin territory of archeological riches. This was an opportunity and a challenge. She wrote the Smithsonian Institution, telling of her education and of her experience in traveling with an uncle who was engaged in research in Egypt. The Smithsonian replied cordially and referred her to the Southwest Museum in Los Angeles. The Campbells became associated with the Southwest Museum, accepting their guidance and instruction.

This was an answer to loneliness, for the urgent need for intellectual effort and accomplishment.

They began their work while still camping at the Oasis and continued it with ever-increasing enthusiasm even while they were struggling to build and equip their homestead cabin. It was remarkable that they could make such progress, for in 1931 the Museum published the first of their "Southwest Museum Papers" entitled, "An Archeological Survey of the Twentynine Palms Region by Elizabeth W. Crozer Campbell."

This book was in Betty's name but the work was a shared enterprise and later publications bear both names. They collaborated but divided their labor. Bill was intuitive in finding sites for exploration. He said, "I look around and decide where I would go if I were an Indian."

Bill fitted their station wagon with camp equipment and extra wide soft tires. He had great skill in driving rocky trails and sandy washes. Betty did the writing and most of the laboratory work.

It had been in the spring of 1925 that they decided to homestead. Bill had received his first pension check; he had been awarded ninety-five dollars a month. It seemed like riches. They budgeted so there was always a surplus to spend on their building. They both worked hard and with great ingenuity. They had a cabin, a well and windmill, even a bathroom with a tub.

The community was growing into a village and Bill was a leader in enterprise. He had recovered his health. They were proud of their own ability to adapt to a life so rugged and demanding. Betty often worked like a man beside Bill, yet cherishing her home and watchful of his health. She was an aristocrat, proud of her family name, happy in her own intellect. Now she was most prideful that she could be a homesteader's wife.

They were beginning to gather stones for the foundation of a room to be added to their house. Then a message came. Betty's father, on his deathbed, had changed his will to include again this well-loved daughter, "a girl born to be hanged."

The inheritance did not come in a great sum of money; it was in the form of a trust with a liberal income. Again they budgeted to build a house, a beautiful home, designed in the style of a colonial farm estate. They used native stone which they personally selected for durability and beauty. This method of building suited their expenditures to their income. They had another purpose; it provided employment for men of the desert during very hard times.

Betty was working as a builder, as a scientist, and as a writer. She was also a good neighbor. She was generous, giving not only money but care and kindness. Sometimes she took in the sick and nursed them.

But she worked too at being democratic — and this was more difficult. She had been deaf from childhood. People often thought that she was rude when they spoke and she did not answer. Unless she saw lips move she would not hear at all. All her education had been in private schools. She sometimes failed to show ordinary courtesy to ordinary people. One homestead wife expressed it, "She was never one of us."

And yet — one morning soon after we came to the desert, I was bathing my beautiful brown baby in his tin tub on the work table in the store. I became aware that someone was watching. I looked up to see Betty and Bill inside the door. Betty was standing with tears running down her face. She was not wiping them away because she did not want Bill to notice.

I remembered that they had lost two babies. And I knew then how rich we were.

A woman Betty truly loved and respected through long years was Ivy Hockett. She was sturdy, like Betty, and she felt pride, rather than shame, that she could do hard work. Ivy also had a philosophy and an understanding spirit. Of anyone who hurt her, and of Betty in her bad moments, she would say, "It's her nature." That was all.

It happened in front of our garage store one day. A cow man, more than six feet tall, approached Bill Campbell with hostile remarks. Bill passed them off, but the man said some slighting thing about Betty. Instantly Bill took off his glasses, handed them to Art Krushat, and a fight was on. The size and weight of the two men was so unequal. A man rushing out of the post office, exclaimed, "We'd better put a stop to this!"

But Art, himself the most peaceable of men, in his twenty years in the Navy had acquired expertise in such matters.

"No," he said. "Leave them be. Bill's doing all right."

Later he told, "I could see Bill kept hitting him at just the right spot by his chin."

The cowboy went down, all two hundred pounds of him, and declined to get up. Bill thanked Art for holding his glasses and came over to our house for minor repairs. I put ice packs on his black eye and offered congratulations.

In the evening both Betty and Bill came to share their joyful mood. Betty was glowing, bubbling like a girl. Her husband had fought a bully in her behalf, and he had won.

Bill, William Henry Campbell, was a leader in the growing community. He found expression for his gifts of intellect, resourcefulness and courage. The Southwest Museum, in recognition of his contributions to archeology, appointed him "Fellow of Archeology" and he was twice elected a trustee of the Museum.

Betty had much cause for pride in the man who, in those first months when they camped at the Oasis, had been so sick that she must not engage him in conversation. But I think that nothing else gave her so much joy as that fist fight in front of Bagley's store.

Doctor Luckie and the Veterans

Many who homesteaded in the 1920s were veterans of the first world war who came to Twentynine Palms because of the interest and concern of Dr. James Luckie.

Dr. Luckie lived in Pasadena where he had a successful medical practice. That phrase, however, coldly describes the work of a man so intuitive and compassionate.

He was a large man, tall and broad shouldered, but his face resembled that of Winston Churchill. There was in his features the same lifelong suggestion of boyishness, of zest for life. In time, Jim Luckie's face became more deeply lined. It is perhaps easier to deal with the fate of millions than with the pain and tragedy of a few.

The men who died and those who returned from "the war to end all wars" were sometimes called "the lost generation." Dr. Luckie knew this generation. Friends had died on the battlefields and some had been maimed. After the first reactions of grief and joy at the war's end, there was disillusion and frustration. This was the frenetic era of prohibition, of inflation, of materialism which belittled their sacrifices and questioned the values for which they fought. They carried scars of lost confidence. Many had asthma, tuberculosis, lungs burned with mustard gas.

Dr. Luckie knew that it was wrong to send such men to the veteran's hospital at Sawtelle, near the coast, to the fog-laden air where they could scarely breathe.

He had watched a brother die of tuberculosis and he, himself, had to contend with asthma. He controlled it with medication but he longed for a way of life which would free him.

Few people in those days thought of the desert as a place to go for pleasure. But Jim Luckie, often with a veteran friend Joe Davis, traveled the Southwest looking for a place where men could find health. They would go for a weekend or a day. They explored mesas and valleys, delighting in the rhythm of the dunes and in the mountain canyons where there was always, on burning days, "the shadow of a rock in the desert land."

They slept under the stars at night and woke in the predawn to watch the miracle of the rising sun. Jim had his own problems and he was burdened with the anguish of others. He realized that the desert gave to him wider horizons and new hope.

He knew just what he wanted to find. It must be a warm dry climate, elevation about two thousand feet, good water, pure air.

One night they camped under the Twentynine Palms of the Oasis of Mara. In the morning Dr. Luckie walked out into the sunshine. The air sparkled. The elevation was right. Summer heat would be bearable, the winters mild. The long basin, surrounded by bare mountains, would not seem desolate to anyone who had eyes for beauty of color and form.

(Dr. Luckie was, like Churchill, an artist. His paintings celebrate the rugged and enduring.)

And in this valley a man could homestead a quarter-section of land and make a home — and perhaps find values to heal the spirit while health returned. Dr. Luckie began to tell patients, "Go out to Twentynine Palms and file on a homestead."

By the fall of 1928 there were enough veterans in the community to form a Legion Post. Men of the Pasadena Post came out to assist with the organization and to install officers.

Bill and Betty Campbell had been building a new home of native rock. It had a large living room, perfect for the meeting. It was still unfurnished but they brought boughs of juniper and pine from the mountains to hide rough walls. Betty prepared to entertain men who were active in the affair and friends of Bill.

The meeting, with its traditional ceremonies, pledges of loyalty and comradeship, was impressive. Bill was elected Commander.

Betty, waiting outside under her athol trees, was tired but happy. To her it seemed a solemn and joyful occasion. She greeted the men who were to be house guests and told them that breakfast would be served at seven o'clock.

To Legionnaires, however, part of comradeship was fun. How good to be free of work and duty on this frontier! They had planned a poker party, poker as it might have been played in a wartime hut. But where?

They went to the Twentynine Palms Inn. The night was cold and so was the host. There was a fireplace but no wood was in sight.

They came to Frank. "After you close up tonight could we use that counter down the middle, and your store?"

We had by then moved our family into a house close by. The store in the building which had been intended as a garage offered novel possibilities. There was a long table down the middle, a pot-bellied stove, and shelves stocked with all sorts of edibles. They sat on sawhorses, nail kegs, crates. They appointed a supply sergeant, named him Nellie: he put a big empty tin on the table.

"Nellie," someone would call. "More crackers and cheese and get a knife. More sardines and get some better ones. Coffee is getting cold."

"Find the Alka Seltzer!" Then coins would rattle in the tin.

They played all night. They could sleep some other time.

Frank had not joined the party. A loss at poker would mean more unpaid bills past due, and he had to open the store at seven-thirty.

At half past six they stopped playing. Someone swept the floor and they cleared up bottles and cans and put them in a carton. They washed under the faucet by the gas pump and looked at themselves dubiously in pocket mirrors. Disheveled, bleary-eyed, but still joyful, they prepared to go and have a good hot breakfast with Betty and Bill.

But to Betty, puritan that she was, the idea that these onetime heroes should have left her house and the beds provided for them and spent a night in riotous living, even though Bill assured her they had only been in Bagley's store, seemed scandalous — an anticlimax to a solemn occasion.

She met the men, hungry, happy, but certainly not at their best. Elizabeth W. Crozer Campbell announced: "Breakfast is served for five and five only — and the five are Mr. and Mrs. Campbell and . . ." She named the three who had slept at the house.

The rejected guests sought frontier food.

Joe Davis, who had traveled the deserts with Dr. Luckie, filed on a homestead adjoining that of Bill Campbell. He had tuberculosis and earnestly hoped for recovery. His friends in Pasadena Legion Post 13 came in a caravan to build a house for him, giving their time and the materials. But before he had regained his strength Joe made a trip to Banning to get supplies, was drenched by a sudden storm, caught pneumonia and died.

Dr. Luckie made it a rule not to charge disabled veterans for his services. Bill Campbell, after he had title to his homestead, said: "Jim, I don't know what I owe you. You won't tell me. So here is a deed to forty acres of my land — and I don't know how much that is worth either."

After Legion Post 334 was organized, the Doctor deeded it these forty acres. There were other gifts designed to make it possible for veterans who needed the desert climate to have places to live. Two neat cottages were built and then a row of one-room cabins such as most motel cabins were at that time. These were the first such accommodations in Twentynine Palms, except for a few rooms at the Inn and at Donnell's hotel.

A tennis court was built and provided a place where we could dance by moonlight to the music of fiddles and guitars.

The community never knew who gave the houses and the court and now it is too late to ask. But in 1931, when my husband Frank Bagley was the second commander of Post 334, he was approached one day by a gentle-mannered man who asked about the life of the community. He asked, stammering, "Wouldn't you boys l-like to h-have a sw-swimming p-p-pool?"

"Of course we would," said Frank. "But it is out of the question. We could not afford to build one."

The caller stammered even more. "I g-g-give sw-sw-swimming pools."

Incredulous and confused by the stammer, Frank could not think he heard right. Excited and afraid that he might fumble, he took the man, Mr. Way, to Campbell's house. Together they agreed to Mr. Way's offer.

He would give all materials and the engineering plans and supervision. The men of the community would donate their labor to dig and construct a modern pool.

It is hard to realize in this day of air conditioning and private pools how much it meant to have a swimming pool when there was no air conditioning and many houses did not even have shade trees.

The men of the village worked with enthusiasm. A year or two after the pool was completed a cement block building was constructed to serve as a bathhouse and office.

In 1934, when the school board managed to finance two years of high school work, it was made possible because they could rent the largest house on the Legion property for classrooms. A year later a second high school teacher was provided; one of the motel-type cabins was assigned for her room.

The bathhouse, also, had various uses. The one-room school-house had been used for Sunday school and for occasional church services.When the State Board of Education ruled that school property could not, under the United States Constitution, be used for religious purposes, C. D. "Cap" Williamson conducted church services in the larger dressing room of the bathhouse.

This courage on the part of Dr. Williamson stimulated the wholehearted community support he received in his project to build the first church, "The Little Church of the Desert."

The veterans, even those who were disabled, had as individuals joined in community enterprises, building the school and equipping the grounds, making roads, digging the pool, and generally helping each other. After they organized in a Legion Post they were even more effective. The Town meetings and the "Twentynine Palms Road Improvement Association" had served well in their time. The Legionnaires carried on.

They expressed the spirit and concern of Dr. Luckie, not consciously, — for many of them never knew him. But it was not only the clear air and sunshine that healed and made life worth living. Men of the "lost generation" were finding themselves.

Years later, after "The Park and Recreation District" was formed, the Legion deeded the swimming pool and part of their land to the district for a park. It was to be named "Luckie Park" and the doctor was invited to be present for the dedication. This was the Fourth of July, 1965. He was an old man with a bad heart; he knew that he was taking a risk to come into the summer heat, but he came.

The dedication ceremony, the tributes telling of his interest and devotion to this community, touched him so deeply that he had difficulty making his response.

The next day Frank and I took Dr. Luckie and his daughter, Susan Moore, for a picnic in the desert mountains where yuccas were blooming gloriously.

He relaxed and gave himself to happiness. He dared not climb the hills but while Sue and Frank hiked the doctor talked to me, reminiscing. He quoted verses he had gathered in his memory during a lifetime. I asked him to write them for me. That evening, when we called to take him to dinner, he handed me some prescription blanks. He said, "I had no other paper. I wrote some lines on these."

I quote here lines from the treasured prescription blanks. He had written: "The thought that came to me when I first saw this valley:

'If scenes like these thy heart can share,
    Then bide a welcome pilgrim here.' "

And, "From an old song —

'For life must come, and life must go,
    The winters pass, the seed flowers grow.' "

He told us, "If they should ever want to put a monument to me in the park, I hope it will be a simple boulder with these lines:

'Here far from noise and turmoil
    May brotherly love prevail.' "

It was his dream — his ideal for the desert town he loved.

Noise and turmoil? From the days of the first town meeting when people parked their cars in a circle and sat on running boards, there has been noise and turmoil. But there has been love too. And I think this has prevailed.

III. Hills and Homesteads

Gold in the Hills
Hughie Leonard's Hat
Hard Rock and Hard Times
The Survey
Final Proofs
Something to Own
A Woman of Courage

Music Valley

Bill smoked in silence, leaning on his shack,
While I gazed wondering, felt it harsh and strange
This waste of sand and sun scorched creosote
Wall rimmed with bones of some old mountain range,
Great boulder heaps, most desolate and wild.
Bill called it Music Valley. He spoke at last,
"The wind makes music in them boulders yonder,
If you will listen when the day is past."

I too have learned to love this desert waste,
These men too restive for the city's yoke,
The men who fight for health, for very life,
The thwarted men, the humble struggling folk.

Here there is love and loyalty and hope,
And courage, always, in the desert lands,
And like the wind in rugged boulder heaps
These things are song to him who understands.

Gold in the Hills

The region around Twentynine Palms was not extensively mined during the period of the Gold Rush. Digging and drywashing in the arid wastes offered no lure to bring men from the streams and the excitement of the "Gold Country" of Northern California.

There is a legend of an ancient Spanish mine. An old prospector known as Hermit John, who had been working in the Sheep Hole Mountains, brought ore into Amboy about 1900. He is reported to have said that he found an arrastra, and a number of graves, evidence that a mine had been worked for hundreds of years. The old man bought provisions and left. He was never heard from again. The "Lost Spanish Mine" remains a legend.

By 1873 there was enough activity in the area around the Oasis of Mara to cause it to be known as the "Palms Mining District." The presence of water and shade made it a natural center. But prospectors went farther into the mountains to dig. An arrastra near the Oasis was used by many miners and some ore was reported to yield as high as $100 a ton.

Miners were taking out much good ore during the early years of the new century. Wages were then $2.50 for a ten hour day and it was not hard to make a profit. Claims were developed in the Gold Park district southeast of the Oasis and Phil Sullivan was in charge of some operations there. He was still working an arrastra near the Oasis in 1927.

The town of Virginia Dale grew up about fifteen miles east of the Oasis where there was shallow water. The director of the U.S. Mint in 1884 issued a lengthy report on the mines of San Bernardino County and mentioned the lodes of Virginia Dale, "from six inches to three feet and yielding well when worked by arrastra." The story of the region deserves a book, not a paragraph. It seems to have been especially marked by misfortunes even beyond the endless litigation and law suits. During World War I it was owned by the Sigafus family of Riverside. It had reached a state of development such that Jim Sigafus was negotiating to sell it for $500,000 but he dropped dead while walking his new pump line.

When we first knew Twentynine Palms there were only a few prospectors in the surrounding hills and one or two promoters at large and active.

The two towns of Dale were ghost towns. The older one had been built of adobe and only crumbling walls remained. Here and there among the ruins lay bits of purple glass, lovely as jewels, attesting by the depth of violet color a half century of gathered sunlight.

The wooden buildings of the second town of Dale stood grey and gaunt amid mountains so weirdly desolate as to suggest the mountains of the moon. There had been a post office and a hotel at the mine. They had been deserted abruptly and had for a time stood empty and open to the winds with bunks made up and long tables set for the next meal.

Dr. Luckie had seen them during one of his early trips of exploration. He wanted to know how this could have happened. One evening when Phil Sullivan was fiddling for a dance in the schoolhouse I asked him for the story.

Phil chuckled. "Wal now, I wouldn't have any idea. Of course they did say the man who run it was postmaster and one night he lost two thousand dollars at poker. Next day he wasn't around. Now I wouldn't have any idee — might have had something to do with it."

Charlie Austin, silver-haired and lame, the first janitor of our school, had freighted supplies with horse-drawn wagons from Los Angeles to Dale. He told me that each round trip took more than six weeks.

During this period the Oasis of Twentynine Palms was a welcome camping place. There was good water from a covered spring and plenty of shade from cottonwood and palms.

There is still a grave under the palm trees. A woman traveling with one of the wagons was going out to the mine to work as a cook. She was taking her eighteen-year-old daughter with her. The girl had tuberculosis; the mother hoped that the dry climate would help her. But the rigor and hardship of the trip were too much. The mother, pitiable in her grief, had to leave her daughter's body in that strange wilderness.

About 1890 an adobe house was built at the Oasis. It was a way station for cattlemen and freighters, then a shelter for any traveler who needed it. It was lived in by some of the early homesteaders while they built their own cabins, and by prospectors, and by the hopeful sick.

Bill McHaney was prospecting in the hills in 1927, although old and nearly blind. He had lived through the old era into the new and when he died in the cold and snowy winter of 1937 he was only waiting for spring to strike it rich again.

He must have been a powerful man when young for although his frame was shrunken it was still erect and square. His face was rugged and weathered like the bare desert mountains, expressing as they do, long endurance of storm and sun. Spiritually, as well as physically, he was native to the land.

Bill had first come to the desert with his brother Jim in 1879. They were cattlemen from Missouri and they ranged and sold cattle extensively. But Bill was not in accord with some of Jim's operations and he soon left him and began prospecting.

Lost Horse Valley, where Bill first prospected, lies along the crest of the mountains which divides the Colorado from the Mojave deserts. There are the bones of ancient mountains laid bare, huge forms of granite, abrupt cliffs, narrow canyons, fantastic shapes. The sand weathered from their sides supports a growth sparse, but rich in variety. Joshua trees posture and beckon, piñon pines grow tall in the detritus of the canyons. Scrub oak and juniper with their delicate color grey green foliage and blue green berries, grow about the crumbling base.

Barrel cacti, which store enough water in their thick pulp to save the thirsty traveler, make bright spots of red against the rocks. In late spring Echinocereus mojavensis is a mound of burning scarlet on the sand, and the beaver tail cacti bloom like roses.

The weird rock forms are not forbidding. Their colors, shading from grey and brown to a creamy terra cotta, contrast with the pure blue of the sky. They invite exploration and they reward the climber with crannies where pines protect him from sun or storm and where needles lie thick and soft. They offer refuge in shallow caves and narrow corridors which are cool in torrid summer.

In winter the snows fall thick. They leave moisture stored around the roots of vegetation and clear water in hollowed basins on the tops of boulders.

This land of beauty between hot deserts must have been a land of refuge and delight to the Indians, but neither its vegetation nor its animal life could support permanent encampments. The Indians were migratory and lived in small groups. Caves offered them shelter. They did not camp too near the water holes for that would keep the game away, nor too far for even a squaw could refuse to carry water an unreasonable distance. Their ollas for water and their cooking pots were of thin clay and when they migrated they did not carry the fragile vessels but hid them in caves or crevices. They marked their caves with "spirit sticks" bare-forked branches standing upright with rounded stones and flicker feathers ceremonially arranged at the base. Squaws ground their seed and grains in holes worn into granite boulders, sometimes two or three near together, for company and gossip.

The Indians of Bill McHaney's day lived much as had the ancient people. He understood their ways and their silences. He did not ask questions. He told Frank he learned that when an Indian voluntarily gave information it would be the truth.

They told Bill where Pegleg Smith got his nuggets of

About 1890 an adobe house was built at the Oasis. It was a way station for cattlemen and freighters. Then a shelter for any traveler who needed it.

Photo by Robert Van Lahr.

Phil Sullivan was still working an arrastra near the Oasis in 1927.

velvety black gold. That was one of the places he wanted to find, but he had put it off too long.

They had shown him gold shining in the cliffs of a canyon deeply hidden in the hills. There he developed the Desert Queen Mine.

Bill's brother Jim joined him and they worked the mine together. It was rich enough to pay well but it was Jim who took the ore to town. While it lasted he lived high. He bought diamonds and wore them not only on his hands but on his hat band. When the money ran low he bought bacon and beans and flour and hauled them back to Bill.

Bill McHaney told Frank that he had insisted on one trip to the city. With the gold he paid off the mortage on his mother's home. In his memory that was the only thing he got out of the mine.

His net gain, however, was more than Jim's. From one of his trips Jim brought back a woman from a sporting house. Bill left them to their ways. To pay for diamonds and perhaps some new machinery, Jim mortgaged the mine. He moved to Seven Palms and his grandiose ways found a new expression. He made lead coins and coated them with gold.

This adventure did not last long. Jim spent years behind bars.

Bill told this story with shame. He had worked the mine for a time after that. The rich veins pinched out in the granite and were lost. The bank foreclosed the mortgage on the Desert Queen.

But for the prospector there was always gold in the hills, solitude, freedom, hope.

When we first knew Bill McHaney he had the use of a cabin belonging to Phil Sullivan during the winter and he had built himself a summer shelter in a place called Music Valley, south and east of the Oasis. He must have built it after he was nearly blind for it was made with brush and pieces of old canvas, scarcely high enough for a man to stand in. But does a man need a shelter when he stands upright?

He told of one day when he was sitting outside on the ground, eating his lunch. Reaching for food he picked up

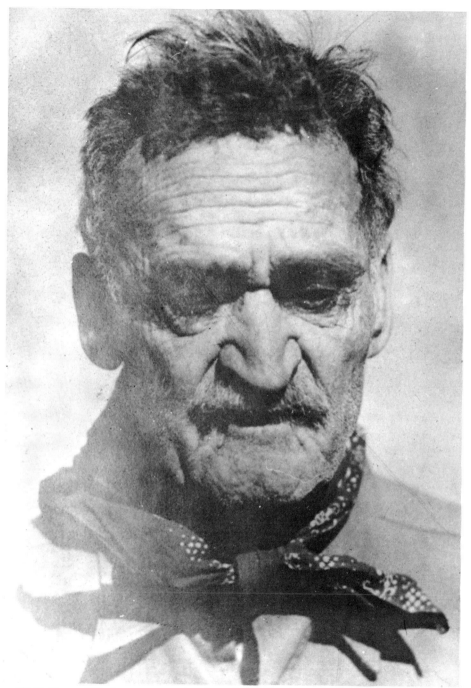

Bill McHaney. "His face was rugged and weathered like the bare desert mountains expressing, as they do, long endurance of storm and sun." He was akin to the land.

something that felt strange. Holding it close to his eyes he made out that what he held was a sidewinder, a small but deadly species of rattlesnake. Very gently he lowered it to the ground and released it. To their mutual relief it wriggled away.

It was of this canyon, rock-rimmed and bare, that Bill said, "The wind makes music in the rocks if a man will listen."

Bill was never friendless for he drew to himself people of many types and backgrounds.

Mr. and Mrs. Campbell, studying archeology for the Southwest Museum, were indebted to him for understanding of Indian life in the hills he knew so well. They were gathering artifacts which were evidence of a prehistoric age. The Indians Bill knew had lived much as their ancestors did and he was gifted with an astonishing and accurate memory.

Mrs. Campbell had the first bathtub in Twentynine Palms. One very hot day when Bill was working for them and camping near their home, she asked him if he would enjoy a bath. He thought that would be fine. She took him in and showed him the towels by the gleaming white tub. Bill touched the water taps. "What are them little shiny things?"

She showed him hot water came from one and cold from another. He said over and over, "Now ain't them the handiest things, ain't them the handiest things."

Fred Jensen was another friend of Bill's. Their common interest was mining. Fred must have looked like a Norse god when he was young. He had been born into the family of an opera singer. He had studied engineering and graduated from Heidelberg University. All of this he had put behind him because he once loved a gypsy. He had little pride left when he came to prospect in Gold Park in the Mojave except in one thing — he had never let his family know that he was still alive.

Fred, with his trained intelligence, recognized and respected Bill's almost intuitive understanding of rock formations and his experience. They worked together one winter, prospecting in Gold Park. They were living in a mine tunnel and Bill grew seriously ill. Fred came to Frank for help and they arranged for Bill to be admitted to the county hospital in

San Bernardino. Mr. Campbell lent his station wagon for the trip.

Bill McHaney recovered. Then came an incident in which he sensed and rejected the humiliation of poverty and Fred made one of the noble gestures which had been his birthright.

Bill was asked to sign an acknowledgment of the charity he had received which would have allowed the county to recover most of the cost of his care from the state. Bill refused and when they insisted he demanded to go home. He was not a charity patient, he said. Perhaps he had no money at the moment but his friends, whom he would repay, would pay for him.

They let him come home but a persistent case worker came with him. For an interview they met, Bill and Fred Jensen and the case worker, in our living room. The problem was explained to Fred. Bill turned to him, appeal in his filmed eyes. Fred rose and bowed from the waist with continental dignity.

"It is true," he said, "that I am obligated to my friend. Unfortunately I am without resources at the time. But shortly, in the spring I hope, I shall pay his account in full."

In his last years Bill lived near the Keys family. They had a comfortable ranch house among the granite boulders; it was a home with children.

He had not used his homestead rights as a young man. Miners seldom bothered to acquire much surface land. Now he homesteaded a beautiful rugged quarter section which adjoined Keys' family ranch.

He came to Frank's office to draw a will bequeathing his cabin and land to the Keyses. Frank said to him. "Bill, is this your idea? Are you sure it is what you want to do?"

"Why sure. Why not? They took me in when I was sick. They even had me there for Christmas with their children. I had forgotten all about Christmas and things like that. I want to leave them everything I have."

Later the Keys property was called The Desert Queen Ranch.

Before the spring Bill closed his clouded eyes. Keys sent word of his death to Twentynine Palms and a graveside service was arranged. His friends gathered in the cemetery and stood waiting in the bitter wind. But the car with Bill's body did not come and, chilled through, we went sadly to our homes.

The next morning another message came. The ranch had been snowed in but the snow was melting. In the afternoon, Bill's friends waited again. At last we saw the panel truck, a laundry wagon, which was to carry the body, come down the road. But straight past the cemetery it went. One of the pallbearers jumped in his car and gave chase. Far down the desert road he overtook the hearse and guided it back.

Bill's coffin was a pine box made by Keys. He had been dressed in a white shirt with a soft red kerchief of a tie. From the shoulders down his body was wrapped in a worn patchwork quilt. His face held dignity and peace.

Friends closed the box and lowered it. One said a prayer. We returned to our homes, but Bill seemed a presence. I hoped that he knew he had been late for his own funeral, — and how many of us had waited there. He would have enjoyed knowing.

Hughie Leonard's Hat

Hughie Leonard was a personality. He was lean and grey and he stooped slightly from the weight of his seventy years, but his blue eyes and his wit still sparkled. In a manner possible only to the Irish he combined an invincible dignity with jaunty gallantry. His speech had only a faint brogue for he was a man acquainted with books, travel, and the science of mining. His suit was threadbare, but he wore his singularly battered hat at an angle almost rakish.

That was a remarkable hat, remarkable for the way in which it seemed a part of Hugh Leonard. After seeing him often I understood its incredible shape. When Hughie addressed a lady he did not tip his hat, he swept it from his head with a grand gesture and held it crushed beneath his arm.

During the years of the great depression, the stringent early thirties, Hughie, using the last of his resources, had turned to prospecting in California. He had a claim in the Pinto Mountains, and while exploring it he lived in a crude cabin about thirty miles from the village of Twentynine Palms. He opened an account at our store which he paid regularly, never failing to say as he counted out his money, "Sure and I thank you for the accommodation."

I enjoyed waiting on Hughie. I was a hard-working grocer's wife, measuring out beans and bacon, but his manner endowed me with consequence and with feminine grace and charm.

Sometimes he talked, relating incidents of mining ventures, of travel, and even of his youth. Listening to his tales I glimpsed obscurely a home, a wife lovely and beloved, and days of better fortune. These were of the past and one did not ask questions of Mr. Leonard.

On his weekly visits, after he had done his trading and settled his account, his recreation was to linger over beer in the small cafe next door. The woman who ran the cafe told me with amusement that in his talk with his cronies he would suddenly become fearful that he might have said something offensive to a lady's ear. He would apologize with wit, charm, albeit with confusion, because he would not know what he had said — or whether, indeed, he had said anything. His drinking was social; he valued it as such.

One day he told me, "Only yesterday it was I had a job, and that for all of five minutes."

"What happened, Mr. Leonard?"

"A little professor is about — very refined and his head full of the learning of books. He thinks to organize a mine and college combined; himself to instruct above and Hugh below with a carbide light for the lamp of learning. Sure and we agreed on the terms and then he said to me, very polite, 'Er — you can't drink, you know.'

"I told him," said Hugh, " 'Perhaps I can't drink, but begorry and you should see me when I try.' "

It was the early days of the New Deal. The paternal hand of government reached even into the Mojave Desert. There was no dentist in Twentynine Palms, and some alphabetical agency set up a temporary office where its clients could go for free dental work. Hugh came to the village with a bad toothache and news of the office was welcome. It would save him a long drive to Banning, sixty miles over rough roads. He went to the office, waited his turn, had a molar pulled.

"I am very much obliged to you," he said. "And how much do I owe?"

"Nothing at all. The government is paying for this."

Hughie laid two dollar bills on the table. "Begod, no government is paying to pull my teeth!" Clopping on his hat at a reactionary angle, he stomped out.

But he was finding very little gold, and although there was active mining in the Pintos it was not easy for an old man to get a job. He was a practical surveyor and developer of mines but not an engineer. More than once he spoke wistfully of "the distinguished position I held for five minutes." His convivial visits to the cafe grew very short and then ceased altogether. When his savings were gone he notified me with dignity and concern:

"It is much obliged I am for the courtesy of you in giving me credit. But if I charge more now I do not know when I can pay."

I told him to continue his account.

"Sure it is a fine thing — confidence." He swept off his hat and carried it beneath his arm until he left the store.

During the ensuing weeks it worried me that he bought so little, and his friends mentioned the meager way in which he lived. He was entitled to the old age pension but it was very difficult for him to accept the idea. "Although," he said reasonably, "my lawyer tells me that as a senior citizen I am entitled to this dividend."

The County Visitor at this time was a woman sympathetic and conscientious. I suggested that she call on Hugh and invite him to apply for the pension. She drove the thirty miles of corduroyed road to his camp and back again. She called at the store, hot, dirty, tired and indignant.

"Why on earth did you send me way out there? That old man has a rich mine and money buried in the ground. He said so himself."

I made an incredulous noise.

She wiped perspiration and dust from her face. "He pointed out the very spot — 'Sure and I always keep a few hundred in a can under that cactus,' he said to me."

I asked, "Just what did you say to Mr. Leonard?"

"Why, I told him that we understood that he needed aid."

The following month Hughie bought almost nothing except oatmeal and tobacco. It was he who worried over his account; I was worried about his diet. When the welfare worker came on her next visit, I told her more about Hugh. She called again at his cabin, this time her approach respectful and businesslike, and he signed an application for a pension.

Within a week, however, he wrote to her office, "Kindly hold my application for the pension. I think I am about to get work." She had gone to trouble enough! She replied that the pension order had gone through. But Hugh did get a job as foreman in a new mining development, and he returned the county check.

Soon thereafter he made a trip on business for the mine to the city of Los Angeles. He came back wearing a well-tailored suit and a new pearl-grey hat of excellent quality. He was delighted with our compliments. But in three days' time, although still lighter in tone, the new hat had assumed the incredible shape of the old. It was no longer merely a hat. It was Hughie Leonard's hat.

Hard Rock and Hard Times

For the old prospectors we felt respect, sympathy, and often affection. They hoped much and they had pride in their work. Soon after we opened our store one made clear to us — though trying to be tactful — that he considered his occupation superior to ours because he developed new wealth, whereas a storekeeper was merely "in trade."

Another man, a promoter, with less tact, referred to our "nickel and dime" business. He had the good will, however, to warn us against doing business with mines. They would want credit, he said, and often we would lose.

During the depression there was a revival of mining in the region. The very names of the mines evoke the perennial quality of hope, adventure, romance which are inherent in the industry: The Desert Queen, Lost Horse, Eldorado, Virginia Dale, Ivanhoe, Golden Bee, Gold Crown, Carlyle, Supply.

The Supply was probably the most productive. In 1931 the California Division of Mines reported that the Supply consisted of nine patented claims and that they had produced $500,000 in gold. The Carlyle and the Gold Crown were well equipped and they furnished needed employment to men of Twentynine Palms and to miners recruited in the cities. They also milled the ore of smaller outfits and made it possible for them to succeed.

There is much gold in the hills of the Mojave and there have been prospectors, like Bill McHaney, who "struck it rich" and for a time became mine operators. Usually the prospector lacked the capital to finance any large project.

After the revival of mining in the '30s many sold their claims to promoters from the city to whom mining appealed as a way to easy wealth. There was a certain Hollywood type, men who were careful to incorporate for only a few hundred dollars. If their venture did not pay, the corporation could go into bankruptcy with no personal liability for debts. They could even evade responsibility for paychecks.

It was fifty miles to the nearest bank and Frank made a policy of cashing pay roll checks in the store, taking all reasonable risks to accommodate residents of the community. "Bouncing pay rolls" were not unusual. He considered them as one of the problems incidental to his business, expecting that they would be made up shortly.

Our resources, however, were small. Sometimes Frank would make a special trip to our bank in Beaumont to bring in money for an expected payday. A week later he might receive word that the checks were N.S.F. and our own account was overdrawn. He would gather up all the available cash from the tills and go dashing in to cover the overdraft.

One hectic winter three pay rolls bounced within a week. Our old friend Jim Byler, recently out of a psychopathic hospital again, happened to be in town. He took me aside and warned me solemnly, "You better look out for that man Frank. He looks like the guys where I came from."

The smallest pay roll, and the most quickly repaid, was that of the experimenting professor miner who in hiring Hughie Leonard had said, "But you can't drink, you know."

The largest was for a mine operated by a young scion of wealth whose relatives made good his labor checks to keep him out of jail. His wife, dainty and pretty, attired in a fur coat, came to see us. She wept into an exquisite hankerchief. "Oh the poor men who need their money. We are so sorry for them. Mark doesn't mean to do such things. He just doesn't add up his check book."

The third mine had been incorporated by high salaried men from Hollywood. Their checks were never fully paid. After a year one of the young miners who had filed his claim with the labor commission received word from the San Bernardino office that money was waiting for him. He took a day off from work, drove one hundred miles to the courthouse, was paid seventy-eight cents on account.

There were other mines, adequately financed, which created a problem because of the turnover of labor. Men would come into town broke, wanting hard-toed shoes, carbide lights, gloves, and groceries. We knew they were poor risks, but they were in real need.

The man who said, "I never leave town without paying my bills" waved a red flag. I can recall only one who having said that, failed to skip — and he was an old miner. The old miner, as a type, had a sense of integrity, and he would settle his account if he had any means at all.

One such, Old Tom, was a problem because his alcoholism was a nuisance. He would go on a spree, get broke, and hang around our porch wanting to borrow money. Sometimes Frank would take him in his car to the other side of the village where he bought his liquor, thinking he might more appropriately decorate those premises. Usually he was returned to us within an hour. After his plea for a loan had been sharply rejected by Frank he would try Hilda Graham in the cafe next door. She was more gentle. "No, Tom, I haven't any money just now."

Patiently he would slouch back to the bench in front of the store where he could keep an eye in the business of the cafe. He would wait until he saw a customer enter and leave. Then he would stagger through the door with careful dignity and lean confidentially across Hilda's counter. "Now you have fifty cents, don't you ?"

When sober Tom was a good worker and so well liked that he could always get a job. Reminded of sums he had borrowed he would cheerfully repay. It was the dubious ethics of giving cash to a drunk man that troubled Frank.

One day, seeing Tom in the early stages, Frank thought he would be clever and forestall the usual requests. When he arrived at our store Frank took him to one side. "Tom," he said. "I don't want it known, but I am very short of money. Could you lend me a few dollars?"

"Sure," beamed Tom. "I've got two hundred dollars in the bank. If it will do you any good, you are welcome to it."

Credit problems with transients were a calculated risk.
Real problems came when our sympathies were involved.

One Sunday Frank was called from our house to the
store, and later I saw the customer driving away with a load
on the back of his truck. We both knew him. When Frank
returned to the house I said, "Did you give that man credit?"

He replied unhappily, "Yes — I did."

"But why?"

"I knew damn well no one else would."

There was always some man like Edwin, hard pushed by
the depression, using every dollar he had saved and risking
his life to work in poor timbered mine shafts. His wife
worked with him, driving a burro loaded with high grade
ore, down a trail perilous with loose rock to an improvised
arrastra. This man, who owned nothing more valuable than
the truck rattling to pieces on the road to Gold Park, saw
fortune as a beckoning light, just ahead, in the humid,
dangerous, ill-ventilated tunnel of his mine.

Nothing Frank had the heart to say would discourage
him. The less he knew about the science of mining the more
certain he was of success.

"Things are looking very rosy," he would assure us
when he came to ask credit for one more load of groceries
and dynamite.

He would put groceries, a can of gasoline, dynamite and
percussion caps, together, in the back of a disintegrating
truck, take his wife in beside him and drive away in the
sunset. Two weeks later he might be back with his sponge of
gold, three ounces, five or ten. The "sponge" was an amal-
gam of ground gold and mercury which had been squeezed
through an old sock, imprinted with the texture of threads.
Frank or I would weigh it for him on the meat scales, wrap
it tenderly, pack it into a tobacco tin or a cap box. Sometimes we helped him to make out the necessary forms, and
mail papers and gold to the mint.

The miner would then charge another load of supplies,
this time with some fruit and candy. He would drive back to

his camp and wait ten days with brighter hopes. When the Treasury check came it was usually for less than half the amount he had expected.

Our literate friend, Fred Jensen, explained: "When their need is so urgent it is not possible for them to estimate the value and purity of the gold with clear judgment." Fred knew. Despite his Heidelberg degree, he was subject to the same stress when he mailed a sponge of gold.

I am aware that gold is so associated with riches that the two words are almost synonymous, and I have been writing of gold as associated with poverty. This is not a treatise or a history of mining. It is a story about a grocery store.

After all this I must relate one bright and glowing exception. It happened during our years of hard times. Frank was working in our absurd garage store. A sleek young man scented with pomade — he was a retired barber — drove up in a shiny truck and came into the grocery.

"Tell me," he said, "where I can find a gold mine."

Frank thought he was joking. "Just anywhere," he said. "About five miles from here. Start digging."

"No, I mean it. Where can I find a gold mine?"

"Well then, go south, young man, go south."

"Quit kidding. Where south?"

"South is that way." Frank pointed toward the road which leads to Gold Park and the Lost Horse country. "Those hills are full of claims. They tell me they are full of gold. Start looking."

"Yes, but just where? I don't want to waste my time."

"Hell! Do you think that if I knew just where to lay my hands on a gold mine, I'd be in this store?"

Three weeks later, on a Saturday evening, he strode into the store, breezy and fragrant. He elbowed through the crowd of socially-minded customers and thrust a two dollar bill upon Frank.

"Here," he said. "Take this."

"What for? Did you buy something?"

"No. It's a tip. You said to go south and find a gold mine — and I did."

When in 1936 the Joshua Tree National Monument was established by Presidential Proclamation there was consternation among those interested in mining. Prospecting and mining of unpatented claims is illegal in National Parks. The area withdrawn was 838,258 acres and included nearly all the ore-rich lands. Mines in actual operation were allowed to continue work, but these were few. In 1950 the boundaries were revised, due in part to pressure from the Riverside Chamber of Commerce. The eastern end of the Monument, more than a third of the whole, was released. The Supply and New Dale were no longer in the protective custody of the U.S. Government.

The price of gold had been frozen; the cost of labor was higher. During the war years the mines had fared badly. There had been gasoline rationing, shortages of material; labor was hard to get and harder to hold. Watchmen would not stay on the job; mine properties were looted for metal and machinery.

No longer can one direct the would-be miner, "Go south, young man. Start digging."

Survey

As more people homesteaded in the Twentynine Palms area the need for a general survey became apparent. Most homesteads were a quarter section, a square half mile measured from a section corner. A section corner should be marked by a stake set in the ground over buried charcoal and plainly marked as "N.E. corner Section 2, Township 1N, Range 9E."

Generally no such stake could be found. There might be just a willow stick lying under a greasewood bush. Usually marks were indistinguishable, worn away by sand and time.

Both Washington in 1855 and A. P. Green, who ran the section lines in this area in 1856, used Indian trails, scrub cedar and cactus for reference points in their field notes, "no other bearings being convenient."

Homesteaders who did have their land surveyed expected to pay not more than twenty-five dollars. That seemed a lot of money to a man who had just paid Uncle Sam sixteen dollars as a filing fee and had to build a "habitable house." Many attempted to measure out their own land.

Frank was often asked for help and his method of using the speedometer of his car to measure the distances and corners of a piece of land was safe enough if the homesteader took the precaution to build well within these approximate boundaries.

But not all did so build, and disputes often arose between neighbors. The neighborhood a couple of miles north of Two Mile Road, along Indian Trail, was sometimes referred to as "the congested area." There was a house on nearly every quarter section. People crowded up like that, with a mere half mile square of land, became jealous of their boundaries.

In 1930 Frank bought a corner ten acres of Bixby's, just diagonally across from the school, the northwest corner of Two Mile Road and Utah Trail. Our store was outgrowing the garage building and he planned to build there. After the deed was signed and the price paid ($100 an acre) Frank said to Ed Bixby, "Now exactly where is this ten acres I have paid for?"

Bixby stepped off some frontage and made a mark with his foot. "Well, here is where I figure it begins."

But since Frank planned to build substantially he wanted to be sure. Bixby understood. He was a grizzled, competent man who owned property in the city, old enough to retire but bored with inaction. They discussed whether any of the local men who did surveying were competent. Benioff had proved up on his land and moved away; Bill Hatch was ill in Pasadena. Frank asked Bixby to consult Howard Way, the County Surveyor, and get the names of men he could recommend. They would then agree on a choice.

Dwight Cooper was selected. He was a sun-browned man about fifty years old, a professional. He came out to see the land. Bixby and Frank were pleased with him. But the price?

"Three hundred dollars."

"Why so much for one corner?" It seemed a staggering figure for ten acres.

Dwight Cooper explained. "For a correct survey I must traverse the township of thiry-six sections north and south twice and east and west twice and apportion the distance between the intervening sections using the San Bernardino Base Line as my base."

Just on impulse Frank asked, "What would it cost to survey the entire township?"

Cooper figured for a few minutes. "I could survey the township, stake out each section and quarter section corner for $720."

Frank and Bixby looked at each other. Frank said, "Are you thinking what I am?"

"I sure am."

"Let's go for it."

Instead of $300 for ten acres that would be only five dollars for each 160 acres. They promptly engaged Mr. Copper to survey the entire township, guaranteeing the cost.

Frank agreed to undertake collecting the price from homesteaders and landowners. Five dollars for a quarter section? It was so little. But not all the land was homesteads and not all homesteads had been patented. He estimated that one third of the landowners would not join in the project. He would try, therefore, to collect enough to allow for that, $7.50 for each quarter section instead of $5.

In his survey Cooper found few stakes properly set with charcoal, many lying on the ground. He said: "In those early days, in such a territory, surveyors were paid by the mile. Often they used a cart with a white rag tied to a wheel, and a compass. The driver would count the revolutions of the wheel for distance and throw out a willow stick at the corners. He was probably thinking, 'Who will ever want this land anyway?' "

Collecting the cost of the survey required almost three years of effort. Many homesteaders were indifferent, a few hostile. "What were those two men trying to put over? And why?"

One man who had grudging paid his $7.50 found four other houses on his land. Fortunately they were small and could be moved. A total of seven houses were on the wrong property.

The largest landowner in the township was Frank Rogers who owned a section of railroad land between Two Mile Road and One Mile Road, adjoining ours. He wrote sarcastically that those little concrete pies would no doubt look pretty on his 640 acres but he saw no need for them. When after the survey he learned that the "City Hall," our water tank, was partly on his land, he wrote again, stern and businesslike this time, demanding that Frank move it at once. He did.

Only Frank and Mr. Bixby had any legal obligation to pay the surveyor. The work was done and the markers in place. It is to the credit of the spirit of the pioneer community that ninety persons paid their share.

Final Proofs

The region around Twentynine Palms had been lived in by Indians, prospected and mined, and used as open range by cattlemen. It was developed as a community by homesteaders.

A government homestead in the desert was usually one quarter section of land, 160 acres. To file: a person must swear that he was single or the head of a household, that he had not previously used his homestead right, and that he had been on the land for which he applied. He must pay a fee of sixteen dollars. He must live on the land for seven months out of each of three years. The first year he must build a "habitable" house. For some time the homesteader was required to cultivate and plant five acres or more during each of the second and third years but in 1930 this requirement was discontinued as being generally futile in so arid a climate.

A veteran of World War I who had served more than ninety days was granted credits for his months of service against his residence time after the first year. A man might leave his family on the homestead as his "principal place of residence" while he went to the city to work and earn money to maintain them. One wife said, "We tough it out." The homesteaders had a saying. "The government bets you 160 acres of land that you can't live on it for three years without starving to death."

It is significant that most homestead plots had been filed three times before being finally patented. A majority of entrants could not stick it out.

To make proof, acquire title, the homesteader must swear and prove by two witnesses that he had lived on the land the required time, verifying the dates, and that he had built a habitable house thereon. A house with a door and two windows, 10 feet by 12, would pass. It need not have a floor or any other luxuries.

When the U.S. Land Office in Los Angeles authorized Frank as a notary public to take final proofs they did not employ him in any other capacity. But people came to him for directions and advice.

He spent hours and days with prospective homesteaders, driving them in his own car across roadless sandy wastes, helping them to find a particular tract which appealed. He gave his time gladly and his love of the desert was infectious. Some of the people he helped were grateful. His skill in driving was notable. He would start from a known location and using the mileage of his speedometer to measure distance, he would survey the boundaries of a section and quarter section. Sometimes he marked the corners of a homestead site by driving a small circle at each corner. He always warned that boundaries so surveyed were only approximate.

But gratitude is not a natural virtue in man. One night Frank guided a new settler who was hauling a truck of lumber for his house to a location near the dry lake. With his car tracks he laid out for the man the boundaries of his land and then he helped him to unload his lumber in a suitable place. While they were working together the man asked how deep he would have to dig to find water. Frank had replied: "Judging from the depth of your neighbor's well. I think you will hit water at about sixty feet."

An attempt to dig a well ended in failure and the homesteader cherished a bitter grudge. He told repeatedly, "That man Bagley is a crook."

The taking of proofs was often highlighted by humor, sometimes by pathos, once by tragedy.

Most trying was a man whose residence had been casual and irregular. He had no record of dates and was indignant that Frank should ask. "I've traded with you," he insisted. "I've bought my bread here when I came. You should know."

Actually these records were verified by an agent of the Land Office who made trips of inspection at irregular inter-

Indians at the Oasis were first Twentynine Palms "homesteaders." Jim and Matilda Pine, at home, 1909. W. E. "Pussyfoot" Johnson, left. Ben de Crevecoeur, right.

In the early mining days, all supplies must be freighted in from Banning or Amboy. These are Frank Sabathe teams.

An old stone building at the Oasis, with tent annex, was Twentynine Palms' primitive first school, Miss Daniels teacher.

vals. He considered not only the written record but looked for
such evidence of habitation as a dump of empty cans, wear on
doors and lintels. He noticed clothes on lines and whether the
same garments, worse for weather, might be hanging out on
the occasions of his infrequent visits.

It was the duty of the notary to ask a prescribed set of
questions and to set down direct and factual answers. Sometimes Frank encountered a witness too conscientious and
literal.

One such witness was a carpenter. He had helped build the
homesteader's house, which was only a short distance from his
own. But when Frank asked this question, "How often have
you seen this applicant living upon this land?" the carpenter
replied, "But I never did."

Frank was certain this was a valid proof, so he insisted.
"Didn't this man live on the same road you live on?"

"That's where I built his house — but I never saw him
living in it."

"Did you see him drive past, going home?"

"I suppose that was where he was going but I never saw
him living there."

Frank: "He has children. Did you ever see them walking to
school?"

"Oh sure. They went by nearly every day. I saw them
walking to school. But I never saw him living on his land."

"Did you ever go there? Did you see a kitchen and a bed in
the bedroom?"

"Oh yes, I saw that all right."

"Hell," said Frank. "You didn't have to put him to bed."

Something to Own

One hundred sixty acres seems a lot of land. A man might work all his life to pay for a farm as large. Of course, in the Twentynine Palms valley it was just sand. But call it a ranch or an estate, it was something to own. It was hope.

Bede Brown was a veteran with foreign service which enabled him to prove up on his homestead after two years of residence. He asked Frank to figure his time for him and to set the date for his proof on the morning of the last required day of residence.

Frank took the testimony for final proofs sitting at an old roll-top desk at the front of our store. He liked to take proofs early in the morning because there were then few customers. He asked me to be on hand to wait on anyone who might come in while he was busy with Brown's proof. He said it would not take long for there would be no dates to figure for time off the land.

Harry Smith and Ed Bixby were to be witnesses.

Mr. Bixby was the first to arrive, ahead of time. Frank was still sweeping the store but Mr. Bixby insisted that he stop and take testimony.

To the question, "Has claimant a habitable house?" he replied:

"Yes, better than most. Brown calls himself a carpenter. I worked with him on a job or two. I'd say he knows his trade, but he won't follow directions. No one hires him any more."

"What other improvements has he made upon the land?"

"Started a garden. I used to see his wife, Connie, watering it with a pail. All dried up now. Made a road, just sand tracks. I suppose she put the white rocks along it."

"Has claimant resided continuously upon the land?"

"Never been away so far as I know. Could have been. His wife has spunk enough to stick it out."

"Do claimant's wife and family reside upon the land?"

"Sure. Two years or more. She'll give you the right dates. Might have been longer; woman doesn't usually change so much in that time. She used to be a teacher, so she says, and right bright and not bad looking. This spring she came and cleaned house for me a few times. Got so she would look like a sliver of brown soap at the end of a wash day. She had to bring the kid along. I couldn't be bothered."

"That is all, Mr. Bixby. Will you wait until you can verify your dates and sign? Thank you."

Harry Smith strolled in, sat down on a kitchen chair, stretched his long legs, hands in pockets. Frank ran through the first questions:

"Has claimant a habitable house?"

"Sure, kinda nice. Three rooms. Connie said it would be their home. She set great store on fixing it up. Curtains and flowers and things. She kept some sort of wildflowers growing."

"Has claimant any other improvements upon the land?"

"Not much to mention. Dug a well . . ."

"A well? That's important."

"Never finished it. Worked so all fired hard on it at first. Connie sure wanted it — tried to help dig. She worked the windlass while Bede dug. Then it was too heavy for her to get up the buckets. She ain't no bigger than a minute. So then she went down and dug. She said she just had to have water for her farm. She joked about it, but it was half joke and whole earnest. Never did hit water."

"I'll write, 'well partially dug.' How often have you seen them residing on the land?"

"Not much lately. She used to have the single fellows in for dinner. Put flowers on the table and make like rabbit stew was a party. She asked me once. Had ham that time and Bede he sat there looking at the carving knife. She says he's nervous. Says that is why they came here and he's better now. I got nervous. Never been back."

"Would you care to say you have seen them residing on the land once a month?"

"Sure, that's O.K. They've been there. She sure deserves that homestead."

I had been dusting cans — and listening. "Bede was nervous." That was as much as she ever told. Many wives complained of homesteading; she never had. She kept herself and the little boy neat in clothes that were worn enough for rags. Lately she had been troubled. I knew that. She was superintendent of the Sunday School that met in the one room schoolhouse. Recently during the class session she went outside and when it was time for the closing exercises I went to find her. She was sitting behind the wellhouse, crying, with her head bent to her knees. She would not tell me why.

She said, "I won't lay it on you. It is my problem. Close the exercises for me, please."

By the time we had finished singing the hymn she was inside the door. She had washed her face from the hose. She smiled and said goodbye to everyone and took her little boy by the hand. He was a good child, but wiggly in class.

"Are you all right?" I asked. "Is Bede at home?" He had been working at one of the mines.

"Oh yes," she smiled. "Likely he will have dinner ready. He came home from the mine last night."

It was rumored that Bede had been fired. That would have been reason enough for most women to cry but not Connie, not like that.

When the Browns drove up to the store they stopped their car by the gas pump and I went out to wait on them.

"We came to make our final proof," Connie said, in a voice curiously small and strained.

She was in the driver's seat with Joey beside her. Bede Brown got out of the car and stalked toward the door of the store. Connie, standing close to me, implored, "Get the doctor for me. My husband is ill."

At the door Bede stopped and looked back at her. He was

gaunt and haggard. Only the angle of his hat reminded me
that when they first came to the desert he had been a handsome man, no older than most of the veterans and usually
friendly.

His wife, too, was pale and exhausted. Her cotton dress
must have been slept in. Clearly enough for Bede to hear and
as though she were continuing a conversation, she said, "And
may our Joey play with your boys while Bede makes his final
proof?"

"Of course," I said, and I took the hand of the four year
old and led him to the house. As soon as he was with my boys I
went to find someone to carry Connie's message to the doctor.
There was no phone; the doctor lived several miles away. I
found Tom Martin working in his garage.

"Sick is he! She's the one who takes enough to make a
person sick. Well, for her, I'll go." He wiped his greasy hands
and left his work.

I watched the store and the gas pump and kept awareness
of the yard where the children played. I went inside the store
to make change. Everything seemed normal. The room was
lined with black paper and when I came in from the sunlight it
was hard to see. Frank was seated at the desk with his typewriter, asking the routine questions. Bede sat near him. Harry
and Bixby loafed in the back. I wondered why they waited
since they had completed their testimony.

I learned later that during the confusion of greeting and
being seated Connie had managed to whisper, "Please stay. I'll
need you."

Bede was head of the family, the homestead would be his,
so it was to him that Frank addressed questions but his wife
often prompted him. He stared straight ahead; her eyes never
left his face.

I went outside and waited for Tom. "Doc's gone to town,"
he reported. "Anything else I can do?"

"I don't know," I said. "I'll ask her."

There seemed to be some need for secrecy so I wrote a
note on the back of a sales slip and handed it to Connie. Bede
seemed abstracted; I thought he would not notice. She took

the note without turning her head but I sensed that Bede's whole frame stiffened. He looked at me and then I became aware of what he was seeing when he stared straight ahead; the meat block, the boning knives, the cleaver.

Doc Foley came in and I waited on him, glad of the diversion. Foley was an older man. short-legged but with powerful shoulders. He had twinkling blue eyes, a mustache grey and drooping and as carefully tended as the little lace curtains his wife used to decorate their car. And from beneath his walrus mustache there issued a voice as sweet and gentle as a girl's. He seemed unaware of the tension in the room, discussing amiably the price of bacon and the dubious freshness of the bread.

Frank was saying, "According to your testimony you have resided upon your homestead two years. Bede's war service in France gives him enough credit to make a third year unnecessary. This is the last day required for your residence." Then, humorously, "Well, Bede, I guess you can swear that you slept there last night?"

"Slept," said the man. "I haven't slept . . ."

Connie put her hand on his arm. "Is everything all right? Can he sign now?"

"Yes, right on the dotted line."

Bede stood up. He scrawled a signature, a sick man's signature. Then he backed away, getting a chair between himself and the company, glaring.

"Men," he said. "Don't kill me. Don't take my wife away — don't kill me . . ."

The man was in terror and torment.

His wife spoke quietly, "Boys, will you help me take my husband to a doctor?"

Bede threw up his arms as though to protect his head, and before anyone could touch him he ran out the door.

"Don't let him go," cried Connie. "He mustn't get away."

Instantly old Foley, with the relaxed manner and sweet voice, was out and beside him. "Feel like a little walk, Bede?" we heard him say.

They were off across the desert, Bede striding, old Foley running a step now and then to keep up.

Connie, her composure gone, was wringing her hands. "Men, don't let him go like that."

"What's it all about?" asked Bixby. "Lot of nonsense — taking a walk."

"Bede will kill him! You don't understand — he has the strength of three men. Oh, don't you understand? My husband is a maniac."

They understood then, in part. It seemed an excitement not too unpleasant, a break in the monotony of living.

"Don't you worry, ma'am. We'll get him." Harry and Bixby piled into Harry's Ford and tore off straight across the sand.

Frank said, "What can we do?"

"Take him into town where he knows our doctor. He must go to a hospital — he can't stay here. We can't go home again."

We could see the men already a mile away across the desert. The car stopped. Foley, in his gentle way, was persuading Bede to get in. Connie covered her face with her hands, but there was no time for tears. To me, she said, "Please put those knives away before he gets back. I thought he would kill you. People writing notes against him — his enemies . . ."

Frank had his car by the gas pump, filling it for a trip to the city. I took him a coat and money from the cash drawer.

The Ford was back with Bede and the three men. Bede was instantly out of the car but he seemed calm.

Connie was beside him. How little she was! "Our friends are going to drive us to town, Bede. We will see your own doctor. It will be nice to have a ride in this good car."

But he would not get in. He came over to the yard. "Where is my boy? I want to see my son."

"He is here," I said, and pulled the child to me. "Can he stay and play with my boys? Children are so restless on a long ride."

"Don't kill him! Don't kill my little boy."

"I won't," I said reasonably. Bede became aware of me.

"Mrs. Bagley," he choked, "you made me and you broke me . . ." He stooped and kissed me.

I had never talked to him except across a counter in the store but in that moment I was someone else, someone comforting. I put my hand on his arm and led him toward the car. "I'll be good to your son. He is happy playing. Just let him stay until you get back."

Bede got into the back seat and Connie beside him, Harry on the other side and Bixby in front with Frank. Connie had whispered, "There must be three of you. He is so strong."

Doc Foley said, "Sorry I can't go with you, Bede, but I couldn't leave without telling my Mommie."

We stood and waved goodbye as though it were a happy trip.

I went back to the house to make sandwiches for the children. Joey had told me, "I'm hungry. We didn't have time for breakfast." As I was slicing cheese he said curiously, "Don't you hide your knives?"

Of that trip to town Frank told me later. They were all back the next day, except Bede.

At first there had been that mood of adventure. After all, Bede was not the first crackpot in the desert. They were sorry for his wife. She certainly seemed scared.

They had driven a few miles, Bede silent, when suddenly he cried, "Bagley, I have sinned. I have sinned before God and against you. I kissed your wife."

Harry burst into laughter. Bixby exclaimed, "Oh, what the hell!"

Frank said, "Let's forget it." But he was beginning to sense the agony of madness. Nothing was funny.

In Whitewater they stopped at a cafe. Bixby went in and brought Bede a glass of milk. Bede knocked the glass from his hand. The milk went on the seat.

They had driven about fifty miles and were in Cabazon. Bede asked in a low voice to be allowed to go to a restroom in a service station. He seemed calm and sane; Frank stopped the car and let him out. As his feet touched the ground he began to run. The three men were after him, tearing down the street of the small town. Suddenly a policeman blocked the way. Bede clutched him, "These men are murderers — save me."

Frank: "Officer, he is sick and crazy. We are taking him to a hospital."

"They tried to poison me." Bede was calm and reasonable. "Just let me show you the car where they held me." He led the way back to the service station. "See all that milk on the seat. They bought it and put poison in it. But I was too smart for them I spilled it. Arrest them, officer. They are murderers."

Harry broke in, "He's as loony as a bed bug."

Connie pleaded, "Officer, this man is my husband. He is insane. Help us to get him back into the car."

Bede: "They will murder me!"

"Someone here must be crazy," exclaimed the policeman. "Get in this building, all of you. Damned if I can tell which one is loony!"

Bixby shrugged his shoulders. "Have it your own way, officer." He went into the service station and sat.

Bede sat down on a pile of tires, his long hands hung between his knees, his fingers twitched from time to time. The officer watched them. He phoned for a doctor and waited. Thieves, poisoners, murderers, maniacs?

Connie, drooping, stood close to her husband, talking gently: "You are so tired, I know. In just a little while we will be where you can rest."

The doctor came in, a grey man with wise sad eyes. He stopped in the door, perhaps ten seconds, surveyed the group. Bixby sitting bored and cynical; Frank and Harry, taut, standing on either side of the door, Connie white, beseeching. And Bede so quiet except for his hands, and his eyes.

The doctor went at once to him. Professional, matter of fact, took his pulse, talked on a few minutes, back and forth. Then in a low conversational tone he asked the group, "Which one of you is in charge here?"

Bixby nodded toward Frank. "It's his car. I suppose he is."

"Come outside."

The officer let Frank pass. The doctor told him sternly: "That man is a maniac. He only wants his chance to kill any or all of you. He should be in a straight jacket. The best we can do is handcuffs. The officer has those.

"To drive without putting him in restraint is to risk all of your lives."

Frank said, "Let me speak to the others."

They came out, the two men and Connie. The policeman went inside the station, close to Bede. The doctor repeated his warning.

Harry's easy grin faded; Bixby's nonchalance was gone. Connie stood there, so small, her own hands strained tightly as though she wore the irons.

"I know," she said. "I tried to tell you. But not like that — oh boys, not like that!"

The men looked at each other.

"O.K., Connie," said Bixby. "Have it your way."

"We will go on as we are," said Frank.

"It is your responsibility. I have warned you." The doctor watched gravely as they got into the car.

Perhaps because he was exhausted by lack of food and sleep, Bede was quiet. They took him to a hospital in the town where he had lived. On Connie's plea he was taken to a room. But when the doctor who was in charge of the small hospital came, he returned from Bede's room angry and adamant.

He summoned Frank into his office. "You had no right to bring that man here. He is dangerous and we have no facilities for caring for him. Take him away at once."

"Could you put him under sedation and keep him overnight? We dare not travel with him."

"No. Just get him out."

"Then may I use the phone?" Frank called the San Bernardino sheriff and briefly told him the situation. "I cannot again take the responsibility of moving this man."

The sheriff called the doctor to the phone. Reluctantly he agreed. "We will keep him until morning."

In the morning the sheriff's car called for Bede and took him to the hospital for the insane.

Connie returned with Frank and the other men in the

afternoon. She came to our house to get her child. They clung together.

"Has Daddy gone to sleep?"

"Yes, Joe, he can rest now."

We urged her to stay the night but she would stop only for supper. The children ate together on the porch. Frank and I sat with Connie at the kitchen table. She tried to eat. She was not yet ready for rest, or for tears, and to tell us was relief.

"More than seven years ago it began. We had been married when he came home from France. He was a good worker, a craftsman. You know he was a craftsman. But he began to lose his jobs. He thought everyone was against him.

"So I said, 'Let's homestead. It will be hard, but it can be fun, too. And we will have something to show for it, our own home.'

"You know how we managed. He seemed better. He didn't talk so much about his enemies. We even had friends.

"But this last week, after they fired him at the mine, he came home and he would not let me leave. I could not go without taking Joey, and Bede would always hold him. He was sly. 'Can't leave before we prove up on our homestead,' he would say. 'They may kill me, you will have this.'

"He tried to hold himself. He told me to throw the knives down the well, and I did. But one was missing — one was missing.

"You know he had guns, a Luger he brought back from France and a 38. I had tried to get him to sell them — I thought he had. Then one day he came in laughing. He had them both. He said, 'Too smart for you, Connie. Look here, all cocked and ready.'

"I thought that was the end, but he began to shake. He knew again. 'Take them and throw them down the well. Be quick, Connie.' I took them and I ran. When I came back he was lying with his face to the wall. He pretended to be asleep.

"I tried to find the missing knife, and then he was sitting on the edge of the bed laughing at me. 'I need the knife to cut our bread,' I said. 'I'll tear it,' and he did with those long fingers and stuffed it in his mouth. It was all we had last night.

"We lay down with Joe between us. I propped my eyes open. When morning came, I said, 'This is our big day, Bede. Let's go and make our proof and this will be ours.'

"He was gentle. He walked around and around looking at things. I washed Joey's face and we got in the car. He let me drive.

"You understand now all I could not tell before. At least, you know enough. I'll never tell it all."

Little Joe came in. "Mama, can we go home now?"

"Yes, Joe, now."

"When will my Dad be back?"

"We will go and see him, dear. We will live near him. It is a pretty place."

"Do they have a well?"

"Yes, and trees and flowers."

After they had gone I turned to Frank. "Will he ever come back?"

"The doctors say no."

"Are you sure the proof was all right? They risked so much to get that land!"

"That's the funny part — excuse the word. The law is that if a homesteader becomes insane while living on his land, no proof is required. They let him have the land."

A Woman of Courage

Few women filed on homesteads. Life was rough for a woman alone. It was an unusual thing therefore when Frank took proof for Ruth Duarte. Unusual, too, was the location of the homestead, near the end of the road in Pipe's Canyon, in the desert mountains, at an elevation of about five thousand feet.

John Olson was her witness. Frank asked: "Are you personally acquainted with the applicant for this homestead?"

"Aye, Mr. Bagley. She come in the summer one day; she say she vant me to help her find a gude place to homestead. Such a little lady she vas, I tink she was a little girl. I tink she joked. But she say she vas twenty-one. So I took her up the canyon almost to my mine and show her some gude land. Aye, I know her."

"When did she first establish residence?"

"Dot must have been September. Yes, it vas summer vhen she come. And she had a house before the snow. Purty it vas then. The squirrels all busy putting avay pine nuts and red and yellow flowers still blooming by the stream."

"Is water available for irrigation?"

"Aye, didn't I say there vas a stream, run right through her land? The snow make it run."

"What improvements did she make?"

"A house. Didn't I yust say she had a house? Carl Yonse, he help her build it. Then he brought his vife and kids. Nellie, his missus, she cook and Rooty teach the kids to read and write."

"Is there timber?"

"Aye, Carl he vas a trapper. There vas piñon pine and

juniper and oak; some big yellow pines too. Sure there vas timber."

"Is the land suitable for cultivation?"

"Vat you say, Mr. Bagley? Vell, in the old country vere I vas a boy ve farm such land. I have a garden in the canyon by the stream, farder down. Rooty, she vas starting a garden in the spring, that vas how she cut her leg. She didn't tink anything about it till it got bad. Then Carl, he took her to the hosptial in San Bernardino. They vanted to cut it off. Rooty made them save it. But it vasn't gude.

"Ven she came back the deer had eaten all her garden."

Frank wrote, "Land not suitable for extensive cultivation."

"Did applicant return a second year?"

"Aye, sure. Rooty she vas not one to give up. I told her the squirrels vere laying up nuts early, and so many piñon pine nuts there vas that year. I told her it vould mean deep snow, maybe tree, four feet. She yust laugh and say she like snow; it yust make her tink of Montana vhere she live with her fadder.

"Her fadder and her mudder vas dead. That vas one reason she vant so bad to have her homestead. And there vas no one to tell her better.

"Carl Yonse and Nellie and the kids they come back again. Rooty's leg hurt her fierce sometimes, but she vould not quit. She said she didn't need a gude leg to teach the kids."

"How often have you seen the applicant living on this land?"

"Oh, I go in and get coffee maybe once a veek vhile the veather vas gude. My onyx mine vas close. I alvays like to talk to Rooty. She like to hear me talk. It made her laugh, and it is gude to hear someone laugh. I tell her, if she ever need me, yust send, I come.

"After the snow came I couldn't drive there any more. It vas about five miles up the canyon from my place. Like I said, it vas a heavy snow, tree, four feet, and drifts."

Frank looked at the clock, but John Olson did not notice.

"Then one day, Carl Yonse, he come to my house. He vant to know, could he get a sled. But I didn't have a sled.

"He say his boy Russ have bad pains, so bad he cry. And a boy like Russ, ten, twelve years old, he don't cry for nuttin. He tink it appendix. Rooty, she had packed him in snow and icicles from the roof, but he get vorse. Rooty's leg vas still bad. So Nellie and he had shoveled half a mile of the road. They tink if they start early they could drive through the drifts. So they go back and put Rooty and the kids in the car.

"The boy, he vas hurting bad and Rooty's leg so svelled she couldn't valk on it. They put in blankets and some grub. The radiator it boil vhen they go through drifts, so Rooty she get out and ride on the hood and scoop snow out of the drifts and stuff it in the radiator.

"They made about tree miles, and then it vas dark. Carl, he made a camp by the car and built a fire in the snow.

"The boy's side vas so cold it vasn't hurting much and he vant his supper. They yust give him a can of fruit juice and in night he kept saying he vas hungry.

"Carl, he kept throwing more logs on the fire and he vondered if maybe his son yust have a bellyache and he vas a damn fool to be camping in the snow. Ya hah.

"But in the morning they tink it better to go to a doctor than to take a chance and maybe be sorry alvays. So that's how Carl, he come to my house.

"Sally, she keeps my house, she alvays vant to feed people. But Carl he yust take some coffee and some bread to eat vhile ve valk. Dere vas a man staying in my house had a big car. It couldn't go up the road through snow, but I told him to shovel out a start and be ready vhen ve come back. I put on my snow shoes and take my scoop shovel and Carl and me ve go back up two miles to the camp.

"Ve say, ve could dig all that road if ve have to, to save Carl's boy, by yes.

"By golly, the Yonses and Rooty, they knew how to

camp, right by the car with a cover and the fire close on the other side.

"I look at the boy and I see him green. There vas no time to shovel the road.

"But Rooty, she look at the two big shovels and she look at Carl and me. 'Russell and I can ride on the shovels,' she say, 'if you and Carl can pull them. Vhen I vas a kid in Montana ve used to coast on scoop shovel yust for fun. But ve have to get out of here now.'

"Then she smile at Russ like they yust going to have some fun.

"So they left their car and all their stuff in the road. Rooty, she not bigger than the boy; they fit those shovels purty good, by yea. Carl and me, ve not very fast, but ve pull steady.

"Vhen ve got to my house my friend he have his big car all warmed up. So everybody got in and they go. They vent to the county hospital in San Bernardino. My friend he say the first road vas rough, but vhen they hit the pavement they fly a little.

"They got to the hospital by midnight. And the superintendent, he remembered Rooty. He put on his vhite coat on top of his pajamas and he took out that appendix himself. Ya ha!

"He told Carl and Nellie anudder half hour and it might have been too late. Aye, a scoop shovel can be a gude ting up in Pipe's Canyon."

Frank, the man, was moved almost to tears. But Frank, the notary, cleared his throat and asked, "Did the applicant return and complete her residence?"

"Aye, sure. She have a gude heart, that girl. Now she have a gude home."

IV. Desert Ways

Sand in My Shoe

The decision to take my three small children to a country as primitive as Twentynine Palms in 1927 had been a struggle. Had I the right, I asked myself, to expose them to the hazards of a frontier with no doctor and no established school — a desert frontier with tarantulas, scorpions and snakes? It was a radical adaptation. Yet a few years later I wondered if I dared take them for a visit to the city.

And the hardships and inconveniences of desert living — they were like "sand in my shoe."

Our youngest, Denny, was four months old when we moved to the desert. He was the only baby in our wide community and as such was the object of much interest. He became known as a "character," a term applied to those original people who add color and flavor to desert life. He grew up with a large helping of the four freedoms and to these he wanted to add a fifth: freedom from clothes. He had been born with a coat of tan that deepened under the Mojave sun to a rich nut-brown. I attempted to keep him in the minimum of garments required by convention, but he learned to remove them before he learned obedience, and even then he remained happily oblivious to the purpose of clothing. When he was two I saw him playing nude with other children near the store. I called to him and said, "Denny, put your sun suit back on."

He picked it up, put the straps around his neck so that what covering there was hung down behind. The children with him did not think it worth-while to change the arrangement. An observer once remarked, "Denny's all dressed up today. He has his pants on."

As he outgrew the privileges of babyhood he accepted clothes if they were cowboy attire.

His imagination made life a high adventure. From the time he could walk he ran away, and he was so small that he would vanish in the greasewood in two minutes. That we always found him before he was indeed seriously lost was due to our big black dog, Mike, his constant companion, who could always be spotted.

But I should not use the word "lost" to describe Denny's journeys. From his point of view it was we who could not be found; he always knew where he was and what he was about. A neighbor who saw him stalking through thick brush, stick at hand and at the ready, eyes front, tried to coax him into his car for a ride home.

"But what are you doing, Denny?" he asked.

"Bear hunting."

By the time he was three he learned to identify tourists as people who asked foolish questions. "Oh, yes," he told a city woman who asked him about snakes. "My father kills them and my mother wraps bacon around them and cooks them for breakfast."

He learned early to distinguish rattlers and the small but deadly sidewinders from the red racers and bull snakes which are harmless. The latter he included in the general friendliness he felt for reptilian life. Once when he was sick in bed he had a shallow box beside him that sheltered a half-grown tortoise and a lizard. The lizard would climb up on the back of the tortoise and all three would nap together.

My own feeling about snakes remained a struggle between reason and revulsion. It was almost more than I could endure when Denny brought a red racer into the house and walked around with it draped across his bare shoulders. By an effort of will I made no protest. I reminded myself that it was clean, harmless, and beautiful. But when I passed through our narrow hall and knocked over a broom that was leaning against the wall I screamed.

Denny said, "What's the matter, Mother?"

"I'm sorry," I apologized. "But that is the way I feel about snakes."

He gave me a sad, reproachful look. Then without a word he took the snake outside and turned it loose.

During the early years I often had to return to the store for an hour after supper, but I would slip home again long enough to tell the boys goodnight. One such evening I found Denny in bed. As I bent to kiss him he remarked, "A snake bit me tonight — but it's all right."

"Where?" I demanded, tearing back the covers.

"On my heel. It's all right. I was walking out near a bush when I felt it strike. I came back into the house and got a flashlight. I hunted until I found the snake. It was only a red racer, so I didn't bother you."

Picnics were our favorite family amusement. On Sundays and holidays, when we attempted to close our store, the only way we could keep it closed was to run away. Our surreptitious packing up and getting away was like an escape from pursuing Indians. Even on Thanksgiving Day when we usually closed at noon, we would throw a few cans of beans, fruit, and bread into a basket and drive into the wilderness. It was infinitely more fun to eat beans in a sunny wash, miles from any road, than to feast at home where customers often called Frank from the table to the store.

There was nothing that Frank liked better than driving where there were no roads. He used two-ply tires and partly deflated them so he could drive through dunes and washes. His feats are legendary even in this era of jeeps. Of course, the boys loved it. The more impassable the route, the greater hero he grew in their eyes.

I shudder to think what we would have done if the car ever broke down for often on that terrain an hour's drive would have equalled two days' walk to get back home with the children. We were lucky that no misfortune ever befell us.

In our explorings we found abandoned mines, old Indian campsites where we dug for flints and bits of pottery, a river bottom uplifted and fantastically eroded like Utah's Bryce, slopes of ancient volcanoes. We would drive all day in this long basin or among the mountains, and never meet another car or see a human being.

When we climbed into the rocks of Rattlesnake Canyon or the Lost Horse country, Frank and the boys would clamber over the big granite formations. Frank could jump like a goat and, of course, the boys aspired to do as well. I had good reason to call my children kids.

We were never so fortunate as to discover a whole olla, but once we found five broken pots of different design together in a cave, and often the boys would come upon an Indian shelter with a witch stick guarding the entrance and marks of smoke on walls and roof. There was one cave in Rattlesnake Canyon where a trickle of water ran overhead, and another cavern, high up, where they dropped rocks into the blackness and never heard them land.

My favorite spot was near Hidden Valley. There in a large boulder is a cavity big enough to hide a small Indian boy on a stormy day. The sides and roof are covered with pictographs. Nearby in granite are two grinding holes. To my feminine mind it suggested a happy, busy hour, with gossip, children playing nearby — and no grocery store.

On these trips we gathered rocks and pottery shards to take home. We admired cactus and left it undisturbed. Some of our friends were making cactus gardens. But I had pulled so many vicious hooked spines from the boys' arms and legs that I had no enthusiasm for them. And I had seen lovely plants, which had glowed red in rocky crevices, wither and die in man-made gardens.

We were not scientific collectors. But along with our rocks and shards we carried home a keen enthusiasm and interest in Indian lore, minerals, and geology. And we had a wonderful time. I am glad that my maternal cautions were so little heeded.

When we reached our own door after such a day I sometimes murmured to myself, "This is really a very superior cave."

Once when Denny was three years old we drove to the high mountains near Big Bear Lake. We stopped under the tall pines and I began to set out our picnic food. Denny was looking up through the trees to the sky. He jumped up and down with joy.

"God," he called. "Come down and have lunch with us."

It was a rare treat when one summer we spent a month under the mountain pines. But as we drove toward home down the back road into the desert, Alan exclaimed:

"Golly! Isn't it good to see some greasewoods again!"

John's point of view expressed our loyalty. We had driven in Yucaipa, then a community of small farms with fruit trees and shaded gardens. It was like the Oregon country I had known, and I said:

"I'd like to live in a place like this again some day."

John spoke indignantly, "Well, I wouldn't. Away off from everything!"

A tradition of our family was a Sunday night supper of popcorn. We had this all through the months when it was possible to endure a fire in our fireplace. Frank was high priest at this ritual which was inherited from his family. The fire must be lighted early to provide a bed of glowing coals. Frank popped the corn kneeling before the coals and enduring heroically almost intolerable heat. There was a ceremonial and sacrificial element in the ordeal. The nearer he came to being a burnt offering the whiter and fluffier the popped corn.

John, the oldest and neophyte, assisted with the fire and tried to endure as much heat as his father. One day a pitying and uninitiated friend gave us an electric popper but it was seldom used. Without the challenge and romance, half the fun was gone.

There was always enough popcorn to fill my largest dishpan, and we ate it from mixing bowls. A plate of red apples and a big pitcher of milk completed the feast.

After the floor was swept we had games and songs. Some of the music we produced was terrible, but there were no neighbors close enough to be annoyed. I wish there were more such music in the world.

Frank was by nature an adventurous man. As a young

boy he had lived on a large ranch in Washington state with five older brothers. He used to assure me that the neighbors had a saying, "You can't kill a Bagley."

Constrained now by the responsibilities of a family and a marginal business, he had not much opportunity to go exploring on his own. But often his work, which included such chores as delivering dynamite, took him into the mining region on the hills.

Once he drove alone into a remote area, followed a trail, and found the mouth of a mine tunnel. Ore, piled beside it, showed that it had been worked and perhaps developed. He entered. The light was dim but he went on, picking his steps on the rough path. Then there was no light. He had a sudden overwhelming sense of danger. He stopped in his tracks. Remembering that there was a flashlight in his car, he retraced his steps to the mouth of the tunnel. He found his flashlight, tested it, and returned. He lighted his tracks on the floor of the passage. Just where he had stopped there was a hole, yawning in the blackness. His footprints were on the edge. He tossed in pebbles but could not hear them reach the bottom. One more step and he would have been lost with no chance of escape. It might have been years before even his car was found.

Betty and Bill Campbell sometimes organized parties to get help in their search for Indian artifacts. Such trips led away from ordinary routes of travel. Frank once joined them.

He loved to be alone in the utter desolation of rocks and boulders. Hunting for signs that might lead to the discovery of a cave, he wandered some distance from the party. Scanning walls of the canyons, he neglected to watch the ground. He stepped on what appeared to be a firm rock. It turned and his foot was caught between two stones. Both were too heavy to be moved by one man.

He was strong and tried to move the stones. He could not budge them. He strained repeatedly to pull his foot free. It was useless. He called for help. There was no

Two phases of Frank.

answer. He heard faint voices, then none at all. Time passed.

The pain was excruciating. He felt in his pockets. Yes, there was a knife, a sharp penknife with a two-inch blade. He wondered if a man could cut off his own foot or would he die of pain and hemorrhage? Desperate now with mounting fear, he gave a final mighty lunge, using his whole body. His foot came free. It appeared to be bent out of shape, like the handle of a cane. His knees buckled and he sank to the ground.

After awhile there was a barely audible shout. Frank answered with all the voice he could muster. Guy Mattox finally appeared, a man who also loved solitude and wilderness. Wise in the ways of the desert, he missed Frank, sensed danger, and began a search for him. He helped Frank back to camp where Betty Campbell built a fire and went to work with basins of hot water. His foot was severely contused but no bones were broken. Days later he was able to walk with a cane.

As Frank learned to adapt to harsh realities of the desert, he made two rules for his sons: Do not walk in the dark without a flashlight, and do not climb in the rocks alone.

It is fortunate that he had learned the second lesson, not to explore alone, before he undertook to find the legendary black gold of the Pegleg Mine.

Bill McHaney had told him that the Indians had confided to him the secret of the Pegleg. He said that when you did not ask them questions Indians told the truth. He had always intended to hunt for it, but now he was too old.

Just go to Borrego, he had said, and find a group of three mounds or small hills. The black gold will be on the surface of the one in the middle, the tallest hill.

It was August. Frank had taken the boys and me to Big Bear to escape the desert heat, and settled us in a cabin for two weeks of vacation. Within twelve hours he was plagued with his old asthma. He had already arranged for the chores at the store and post office to be handled in our

absence. I urged him not to go back to work. I knew he
needed a change. "You have always wanted to go prospecting," I said, "and it will be cool in the mountains around
Desert Queen Mine."

But he set out to find the fabled "Pegleg." Jim Graham,
our desert neighbor, was a kindred spirit. They made themselves a rough map from all the information that Bill
McHaney could remember, and drove to the Borrego
Desert south of Indio. Even the attendant at the service station where they stopped to fill up protested, "This ain't no
time of year to go in there!"

There were many groups of three mounds. They explored several. In the afternoon, around three o'clock when
temperatures soared to 120, Frank climbed to a higher hill.
He scrambled over rocks that covered the slope. He was
tired but kept going. He thought of the possibility of sun-
stroke, but he was sweating freely, had water in a canteen,
and believed he was safe.

Suddenly he began to cramp. He sat down to rest and
drank some water. His body rejected it. He tried to get up
but cramps forced him to the ground. He could crawl but
he could not stand.

Jim saw that something was wrong and quickly came to
him. He made a spot of shade by spreading a piece of muslin, which they had brought to carry their gold nuggets, on
the stalks of an ocotillo. It protected Frank's head from the
sun. Jim descended the rocky slope and brought back more
water and a can of soup. Nothing would stay down. Frank
vomited and cramped unceasingly. Rest did not help, nor
the cooler air of sundown.

Telling of it afterward, Jim praised Frank's grit and determination and marvelled at how he crawled over sharp
rocks and cactus thorns. Frank told how Jim carried him.
After dark they managed somehow to get down the hill and
cross the several miles of desert to the car.

When they reached it, Frank said weakly, "Take me to
Banning. We can go to a hotel."

Jim drove across rough ground, picking his way through

the badlands by retracing their own car tracks. When Jim found the highway, he drove straight to Indio and pulled up at the hospital.

Frank asked, "Is this the hotel?"

Jim said, "Yes," and disappeared in search of the doctor.

When he arrived at Frank's side, the doctor studied his pale, clammy face, and checked his pulse.

He said, "Let's get this man inside as quickly as we can."

Hospital personnel understood heat exhaustion and were prepared. They laid Frank on a table and presently a flask of saline solution began to drip through a needle into his blood stream. The cramps slowly subsided.

When Frank was discharged in the morning, he asked the doctor, "What would have happened if we had just gone to a hotel?"

The doctor answered, "You would have died."

It now seems incredible that heat exhaustion was generally so little understood or respected by desert dwellers in those days. Now we know, of course, that it is caused by loss of body salt through perspiration and can be prevented by taking extra salt with water. Thanks largely to experience gained when Hoover Dam was built in the canyon of the Colorado River, it has long been common practice to supply salt tablets to men who toil in desert heat.

When the two men reached home and I had heard the story, I went to Jim to thank him.

He said, "I could not see myself coming home and explaining to you and the boys why I had left him there."

The Fallen Star

It happened when Alan was nine years old — there appeared on our western horizon a new star — a Hollywood star.

Alan was spiritually attuned to the worship of heroes, and to him heroes were associated with the stars — but with the brilliant, beautiful constellations which we saw from our bed on summer nights. For our village on the desert frontier lacked the cultural joys of movies and television, and our small house was like an oven in the summer months. And so we put a row of five cots in the yard and we went to bed early. The grey dusk was tender and comforting. The three boys and I were usually in bed in time to see the first stars appear. Frank often came to rest in the cool dark as soon as he could close the store. It was he who taught the boys to recognize the summer constellations and told them the Greek myths about the heroes enshrined forever in the stars.

A flier in the first world war, on the training fields of Texas, Frank had learned to know the stars as guides, and from college days he recalled the myths of Greece.

By day, the boys knew him as overworked and worried — often impatient and stern. He seemed a different person when he talked about the stars. He told of Perseus of the winged feet, of Hercules who performed the seven mighty labors and who chose to die upon a funeral pyre rather to live diseased and dishonored. Denny might go to sleep, for he was only a little boy, and John would doze off in spite of himself, for at twelve he was large and strong and worked and played exhaustingly. But Alan, who was attuned to the music of the swinging skies, and to the songs of heroes, would listen entranced until in the starlight we would see him propping his eyes open with his fingers. "Tell me more about Hercules, Dad."

By day, Alan was rather afraid of his father. They had never been very close.

And then there appeared on the horizon of our lives a Hollywood star, a western hero, who by the brightness of his virtue caused the heroes of mythology to pale. And not only those Greek half-gods, about whose private lives one does not tell too much, but also such noble characters as David, who was handy with rocks but knew nothing of lariats, and George Washington, whose father would probably have licked him if he had not told the truth — these too faded into obscurity.

This new hero was named Jo Elk. He had been a cowboy riding the western plains; there was in his blood a trace of the noble red man; he had become a movie star because he could out ride, out shoot, out lasso any other cowboy on prairie or screen. He was, moreover, a shining example of manly virtue. The label on "Winsall Cereal" said so.

Alan cut out the label and mailed it. He was rewarded with a booklet which told how to form a club, the Square Shooter's Club, devoted to the study of his life and to the qualities of manliness, steadfastness, courage, which he, in his handsome athletic person, exemplified.

Five labels, sent in by as many boys, were required to earn an embossed charter for a Square Shooters' Club. After much extolling of Winsall Cereal, Alan persuaded four friends to send in labels with his. They received a scroll bearing a picture of Jo Elk mounted on a white stallion. Below the picture were printed the ideals of the club:

"Be honest in word and deed
Be clean in body, mind, and speech
Be steadfast — never give up
Be brave — and so be strong
Be a Square Shooter."

Alan, as founder, was head of the club and the charter hung in his room. Serious little boys tramped in and out and the membership doubled. But this arrangement had drawbacks. George Brown, a sober child, had been elected secretary-treasurer. He protested:

"Where Alan hangs the charter is John and Denny's room, too. John is a scout and he ain't respectful, and Denny is just a little kid. Besides, Alan's father sells Winsall Cereal in his store. This makes it seem like advertisin'. It ain't fittin'."

Alan said, "I wouldn't want to do anything that makes our club seem cheap."

After a week or two the boys resolved to settle their problem by building a club house. It was voted to build on our homestead, which was central in the scattered village. Alan approached his father on the subject of a deed.

"We want to put it far enough down the hill so it will be out of sight from our house. We don't want it to be part of any yard. I'm supposed to ask you — sir."

Frank blinked at the "sir." "I don't want any litter of boxes and rubbish on the land, not even out of sight."

"Oh no, sir. We are going to build sound and square. We voted to earn the money to buy all new lumber; we don't want anything junky or secondhand."

"How much land do you require?"

Alan summoned his courage. "Five acres will do."

"I'll give you a paper that says you have undisputed possession for purpose of a club."

The building of the club was the project of a summer, for the kids earned the money for it, and small boys do not pick money from creosote bushes.

Alan was a slender youngster, sensitive, quiet — and lazy. Now he worked "steadfastly" at any task he could find to do, and he deposited his earnings, to the last penny, with the treasurer before he could be tempted to spend them. He developed a surprising ingenuity in getting jobs for his fellow members. When he asked to be allowed to help in the store without pay, to sweep up and sack potatoes and carry out boxes, his father could hardly believe his senses. Then he observed his son standing beside the pop case when his friends came in, standing silent but stern, to see to it that they did not waste their nickels in riotous living.

As soon as the treasury held enough money to buy cement the boys laid the floor. They had to carry water in pails from our house and mix the cement by hand in an old wash tub. They could easily have gathered enough scrap lumber and boxes to build a shack, but they stuck to their resolve and bought all new lumber. The walls were of boards set vertically, the roof was shed type. There was one small window, and one door, which had a lock. But the structure was sound; it would not blow down in the desert gales, and it was set four square with the compass.

George's father, Bill Brown, who was a carpenter, had taught the boys how to tie studs and joists together and how to brace the corners. His son proudly quoted. "We don't want anything flimsy for a Square Shooters' Club — it wouldn't be fittin'."

"It's not very big," said Alan. "I'll bet Jo Elk could get his lasso around it, but he couldn't budge it off that foundation."

Mr. Brown was elected honorary leader of the club. He was a gentle, worn little man, but he had once worked on a ranch and admitted to having thrown a lasso.

I heard George and Alan talking.

"Maybe my dad never lassoed wild horses like Jo Elk," said George, "but he says he reckons he was pretty good."

"My father can shoot better than any of the other men in town," said Alan.

"Tin cans!" said George. "Why don't he hunt?"

"He doesn't like to kill things," Alan apologized.

I wanted to put in a word about war, and how Frank had learned to shoot, but I kept to woman's place — the kitchen.

George's father had time to accompany the kids on weekend hikes. No one was afraid of him. The boys really ran the club themselves, and that was the best thing about it.

Being the middle child in a family does not encourage

self assertion. Yet Alan developed initiative and courage. He had always feared pain, but when he broke his arm — practicing cartwheels down a hill — he chose to have it set without anesthetic. White and drenched with sweat, he tried to grin encouragement at me.

George, too, was changing. A sober child, seeming to lack the imagination to make him a worshipper of heroes, he took seriously the ideals of the charter: be clean, never give up. Although his home was a desert cabin where water had to be hauled in cans, for the school year after the formation of the club, George won the teacher's prize for being the cleanest boy in school. His fair skin was always pink with scrubbing, his blond hair always brushed smooth. School had not been easy for him, and reading had been especially difficult. But during that year he turned in more reports for books read than any other child in his class. His reading led him into a new world, peopled with heroes. But Jo Elk was nearer. He was alive, he had lived in a world like our desert. Like a star which is low on the horizon, he was magnified by the atmosphere of earth.

Most boy's projects are abandoned after a few months, but the Square Shooters carried on for a second year. It meant a great deal to the boys because they had a club house and because it was their own.

The Winsall Cereal Company did a good job as sponsors. We all got rather sick of eating the breakfast food. Frank grumbled, "Reminds me of the hay I used to bale." But for additional box tops there came material for play. A fancy lariat and a book on rope tricks cost five tops and fifty cents. For just two tops and one dime "to cover mailing costs" a member could get a shining silver star to wear in his belt. From time to time, on the packages, there appeared new chapters in the story of the valiant Jo Elk.

And then we had an opportunity to see this hero, not in pictures, but in real life. Jo Elk had lent his name and fame to a small circus. On Thanksgiving Day this circus would be in Riverside. We saw Alan studying the advance publicity in the newspaper. His dark eyes were shining. It was Frank who said, "Let's go!"

He would have to close the store, and our country customers always took the closing of the store, even on holidays, as a personal affront. He would have to drive one hundred miles and back, and he couldn't afford it. But we were going to the circus! It would be a rare and wonderful treat. None of the children had ever seen a circus. And — Alan would see Jo Elk.

We would leave in the morning, eat a picnic lunch on the way. After the show we would have Thanksgiving dinner in a restaurant. It was to be a special treat for me too.

We were sorry that we could not take all the club members; we invited George to go along. He appeared, dressed immaculately, his blue jeans freshly washed and ironed, his shirt dazzling white, the silver stars in his belt polished to gleam. Alan never did look like that; I told myself it was because he was so dark. But he was brushed and scrubbed and he had without argument put on the best clothes he owned. The stars in his belt had been polished so hard there was not much silver left, but they shone.

John and Denny were trying to hide their excitement. John had always assumed an air of superiority toward the club, and Denny had expressed his envy and admiration by being a pest and a nuisance on occasion. But they both had more respect for the Square Shooters than they cared to admit. After all, Jo Elk was a living person, dashing and handsome, and it was something to be a charter member of an organization which ran itself. They had eaten a lot of Winsall Cereal with less crabbing than was to be expected.

There was glamour and rousing music as we filed through the door into the big tent. We looked for our seats. We had paid an ordinary admission, fifty cents each; our benches were so far at the end of the tent that the main ring would be scarcely visible. Frank pulled out his ten dollar bill and bought six reserved seats at one dollar each. George and Alan stared, but they soon forgot.

The reserved seats were good enough. The band played

short, lively pieces, changing tunes at the sound of a whistle. Then came the parade; clowns tumbling and chattering, girls whose rouge made them look older and harder than they really were, lions in cages they could easily smash if they had the energy. By this time I realized just how second rate this circus would be, but I hoped the kids would not know. And then — Jo Elk!

He rode a beautiful horse, just like the pictures, a white horse, its saddle and bridle loaded with slightly tarnished silver. But the hero himself, the star — he looked like a washed-out roué.

I looked at the Square Shooters. They were clapping loudly. Alan and George were standing. But Jo Elk, although he was bowing to the stands and waving his wide white hat, was too bored to notice boys.

He sat in the center of the ring for a few minutes, behind the ringmaster, before he disappeared. The clowns cavorted; the painted girls galloped around on wide-backed horses. The old lions snarled at the trainer with the whip and the threatening chair, climbed on their stools, and yawned. There were cowboys too, of course, they did some rather good rope tricks. But Jo Elk did not take part.

Something had to be done to make the show an occasion. Frank extravagantly bought soda and popcorn of the vendors. Denny was still wide-eyed. John scoffed, "Where's our hero? Why doesn't he come back?" I jabbed him with my elbow. Alan and George said nothing.

"And now," proclaimed the ringmaster, "with this act our show ends. But by special arrangement the great cowboy actor, Jo Elk, will give an exhibit of his incomparable skill in roping and shooting." He barked on, "A stupendous — hair-raising — command performance — kings and queens of Europe — Ladies and Gentlemen, for only twenty-five cents — one small quarter — you may remain."

The ushers appeared with tickets. Alan turned toward his father, "You don't have to, Dad," he said.

Frank dug into his pocket again.

Only a handful of spectators remained, and we were free to take the best seats in the house.

He rode into the ring, this burned-out, middle-aged man in black and silver, on his beautiful white horse. He swept off his hat, gestured vaguely toward the reserved seats, but he did not bother to make his horse prance. An attendant in western attire — he at least was lean and brown — handed up the silver mounted gun. The target was a wheel of six colored lights, revolving at the end of the tent. Jo Elk shot six times — the band blared — the lights went out.

The star bowed and dismounted. The lean young cowboy caught the reins of the horse and twisted cruelly at the heavy bit to make him rear. A girl in red satin briefs, western-style, handed Jo Elk a lariat; another girl, really slim and quite pretty was turning cartwheels and handsprings at a distance of about fifty feet.

"Ladies and gentlemen," trumpeted the ringmaster, "Jo Elk, who has roped wild horses on the plains of Texas, Arizona, Nevada and California, will rope the feet of this little filly, who is swifter than any gazelle of the prairie."

The girl turned cartwheels with easy grace, about as slowly as cartwheels can be turned. Jo twirled his rope, he tried once. And then he turned and walked off stage.

The band blared and packed up.

It was five o'clock, the wind outside was cold. The rickety wagons with the old lions were already on their way. The cowboys and the clowns, helping to pull up tent stakes, were cursing the wind and dust. The ground was littered with bottles and trash, bits of dirty paper flew in our faces.

After the unexpected cost of the show, turkey dinners were not to be considered. We found a lunch room cheap enough to serve hot dogs on Thanksgiving Day, and arranged ourselves around a white glazed table.

The Square Shooters were tired and quiet. Not even John and Denny kidded them.

But after the first mouthful of meat and mustard their spirits lifted. George, the serious child, looked up. "My Dad wouldn't rope a girl," he said, "it wouldn't be fittin'. But he wouldn't quit with one try."

With the thought of the gentle Mr. Brown "steadfastly" trying to rope a girl, we relaxed in noisy laughter. George joined in, pleased and surprised that he had been funny.

Alan spoke to his father across the table. "I suppose," he said slowly, "some of the old guys were like that — Hercules and David and those guys — not all that they were cracked up to be. I suppose it doesn't really matter."

"Sometimes," said Frank. "It doesn't change the verities."

"The very-tees?" The word was new, but Alan understood. Then he grinned broadly. "There's one thing to be thankful for, Dad," he said. "You won't have to eat any more baled hay."

He hesitated, then added shyly, "He wasn't a bit like you."

Credit Account

When our son Denny was five years old he began to put away childish things and to become a very practical and responsible person.

At three he had boldly stated, "I was born a cowboy." And not long after, having been teased by his older brothers, he had confided to me. "When I say moo like this, 'Moo-oo-oo' — even when I know it's me, I'm scared."

But after he was five he no longer told me wild yarns in the first person or went wolf hunting in the sage brush with a wooden gun. Certainly he was no longer scared by his own moos. And he asked me for a job.

"I'm old enough to earn my money," he said, "Gosh, mother, you shouldn't be giving me twenty-five cents every week."

So he was assigned a job. He was to water the athol trees and oleanders around the house, rake the yard, carry out garbage and papers to the hole where they were burned, and to continue to run errands.

Our family life in the Mojave desert was not easy. The other boys, two stair steps up from Denny, had their duties. Men who have driven ten or thirty miles over sandy roads from homestead or mines expect service at any time, and store hours were long in Twentynine Palms.

Although the nearest cattle ranch was twenty miles away at Warren's Well, the country between was open range and cowboys with worn chaps and bright kerchiefs often rode through the homestead community looking for strays.

Denny's interests naturally focused on western lore and on horses. He always wore cowboy clothes, not the fancy things that come in a box, but plain blue jeans and plaid cotton shirts. Because he was a slim and strenuous little boy, the jeans slipped down and his shirt tail was always out. Eight months of the year he went barefoot and he walked everywhere. His small feet usually lacked a toenail, and the soles were like leather. A range rider might have envied his tan, for he was born with one coat and in five years he had acquired five more. When he grinned his teeth flashed white; fortunately his hair was straight and his eyes were blue.

It was almost inevitable that, having become a responsible person with an earned income of twenty-five cents a week, he should begin saving money to buy a horse. At first the horse was a grand, remote objective. For hitching purposes it was about like a star.

Nickels slipped away for ice cream and pop, but by the time he entered school his savings amounted to a few dollars. Then came larger temptations. For ten box tops and one dollar Jim Rogers would send one genuine huntsman's knife. Denny struggled over the problem, discussing it soberly while he wiped the supper dishes. He did not talk just horse, he talked knife and horse.

"I've learned enough arithmetic to know it will be years before I can buy a horse. Gosh! I've got enough for a hunting knife."

The decision was his. When the box tops had been sent I guessed that it was so because we were permitted another cereal in the house. The knife came, but it was not the true steel a six-year-old frontiersman needed. The blade broke, the dollar was gone.

We talked horse again. One evening I remarked, "I hope you may be a rancher when you grow up. You love animals and outdoors so well."

"Okay, if you think I should. But nothing that has anything to do with trees or garbage."

The reply was not intended as complaint, and since there was no smaller brother to whom his job could descend, he was not relieved of it. Other duties were added as his brothers graduated to work around the store, and his pay was increased.

He made another business proposition, "It's too easy for me to get at the money when I keep it. With customers so slow about paying their bills you need it. Why don't you take care of my money and you can use it until I get enough saved."

The idea was sound. A credit account was opened at the store in Denny's name. There was no bank nearer than Banning and people who had a little money sometimes had us keep it for them in that manner.

A Sears Roebuck catalog, full of wonders, arrived by mail. Denny's longings settled on a pair of roller skates — two dollars and twenty-five cents plus postage. We reasoned together that the only cement available for skating was the short walk in front of the group of buildings at the business center, store, lunchroom and garage. Because he was the son of a proprietor he would not be allowed to skate there during busy hours. But he drew from his credit account and sent for the skates.

They were not very good skates and they had rough use. One day Denny appeared in our back room office, his nose smudged with grease, his brows furrowed. "Mother, how do you write a business letter?"

"Tell everything exactly and make it as short as you can."

He borrowed a pencil and sheet of paper and stood across from me at the desk. Frowning in concentration, elbows on the table, his tongue caught between his teeth, he labored mightily. Now and then he would sigh, relax by rubbing one brown foot against the other, erase, then try again.

He wrote:

"Dear Mr. Sears,

2 weeks ago I bought a pear of skates which cost $2.25 not counting postage all together it was $2.42.

It broke beyond the fixing of our local garage. If you can fix it alright if you can't just send them back and tell me what it cost.

Denny Bagley"

Mr. Sears did not respond. The credit account was short $2.42.

It was about this time that Ben Richardson brought in a string of riding horses. Although most of them were badly broken or dispirited there was one little bay with a white nose, gentle enough and lively enough to win the heart of a seven year old. Her name was Lassie. During the few months that the pony was in the village all Denny's current income was spent for rides. He learned to handle a horse rather well. So far as I know, the only time he was ever thrown he went over the pony's head and landed squarely on his bare feet.

But the patronage of the riding stables was not sufficient. Ben Richardson left for a larger town and took Lassie with him.

Facing this problem Denny wrote another business letter:

> "Dear Mr. Richardson,
> If you wood sell Lassie and if I can save the money how much wood she cost? And do you think you will be back next year and still have her?
>
>   Respeckfully,
>   Denny
> P.S. I can't get it for another year."

The reply was prompt. Lassie's price was forty dollars. She was a good pony and would remain in the string until next season. Mr. Richardson would see Denny then.

Denny's birthday was in June; because he was all of eight years old and a man of affairs his father gave him five dollars. For two days he carried it around, but then he deposited it, observing sagely, "Gosh, when I had just twenty-five cents, all I could think of was spending it. But now that I have fifteen dollars I don't want to break it."

Pocket money still slipped away. The swimming pool was a joy and a necessity in summer and swimming makes a boy hungry for hamburgers at odd hours. But Denny did not draw out any capital. He planned that in seventeen months, in the winter of the year when he would be nine, he would have enough for the pony and ninety eight cents (Sears Roebuck price) for curry comb and brush.

Other considerations entered his thoughts. What would it cost to feed the pony, how much to buy lumber for a shed? "I'll make it myself, you won't have to help me with anything except maybe the roof."

His father told him that we would expect to pay for the feed and lumber but Denny was sobered and somewhat worried when he realized that we would have to pay out as much as the price of Lassie.

It was a keen disappointment that Ben Richardson did not bring his string of horses to town that fall. The Heelys brought in horses and Denny treated himself to a few rides at fifty cents an hour, but there was a troubling sense of disloyalty when he spent money on another pony, money he could have saved for Lassie.

In the spring the riding stables held a rodeo of games, prizes to be paid in silver coins. Here, thought Denny, was his chance to win back part of what he had squandered! But horses were assigned by lot and it was his bad luck to draw a rangy, disillusioned, long-legged beast. The games, potato races, musical chairs, short races, all involved repeated mounting and dismounting. Denny, though wiry, was small for his years. Getting off was easy enough but every remount was a struggle. Desperately serious, stretching until his brown back showed between his jeans and red plaid shirt, he would scramble up the stirrup and into the saddle. The home town crowd laughed and cheered the smallest boy on the biggest horse, but he finished last in every contest.

When we left the rodeo to go home he looked so utterly fagged and dejected that even his brothers cut short their teasing. I said, "Never mind, it was just your bad luck that you drew the tallest horse."

He was of sterner stuff than I. "That isn't any excuse."

The following summer was unusually hot. The town's embryo Chamber of Commerce boasted of "the all year climate." Off the record, old-timers said, "The all year climate, hot in summer, cold in winter."

When the mercury climbed to 114 degrees in June everyone with money enough to escape the desert did so. Many of the customers who were left to us were unemployed and seemed content to sit out the summer on the shady side of our store. They became, in a sense, our summer boarders. The weather was a disaster to our business.

On Denny's ninth birthday we gave him only one dollar and he promptly turned that back into his credit account.

The long hot days were a physical strain. We had no air conditioning. The nights were tolerable because we slept in the open, but they were too short to allow the rest children need. The boys swam too much, for only in the pool could they play without becoming exhausted by the heat. Denny learned to dive expertly and by the time summer ended he could do a jackknife, a backward flip and a one and a half. He sunburned to an odd purplish hue. But he was thinner than ever and he developed an ear infection.

Cool weather of the fall was welcome, but winter came early with cold harsh winds. All three boys were sick and Denny had pneumonia. Their beds were moved into the living room where there was a fireplace for warmth and ventilation. Their father kept up roaring fires and I made mustard plasters and slapped them on — one — two — three.

As soon as Denny was out of bed he took up his chores and he resented any suggestion that he rest. His reaction to being the youngest of three brothers and smaller than his friends had always been a stubborn drive to keep up, to compensate through will.

Turning again to business matters he brought his book of account from the store. Carefully added and subtracted, and he looked up with his old-time grin.

"Gosh, mother, in one month I'll have enough!"

He wrote a letter to Ben Richardson, and without waiting for an answer he sent to Sears for a curry comb and brush.

Ben Richardson answered kindly and promptly. "Lassie has a few grey hairs but she is a good little mare. Her price is still forty dollars."

Denny consulted me as I was preparing dinner. "Forty dollars is a lot to take out of your business all at once. Suppose I start now and take it out ten dollars a week?"

Busy with hamburger and vegetables, I delayed an answer. I was figuring too, dollars and cents — and something more vital. Denny's estimate as to the condition of our store was funny, but not very funny. Forty dollars, however, did not look as large to me as to him, and balanced against his hope and determination it had no weight.

But he was not a well child. His father and I were worried that he regained strength so slowly. If he had the pony he would rise early and go out into the winter wind to feed her, carry water and clean the stable. It would have to be his responsibility and he would not want it any other way. I could not tell him he was not strong enough.

"Denny," I said, "the money is your own, you can draw it when you want it. But how much did you say the shed would cost?"

"The lumber man and I figured it. Thirty-seven dollars and eighty-nine cents."

"And the feed?"

"The stable man and I figured that, three-nineteen a month. Gosh! That's a lot of money, isn't it!"

I kept silent, chopping apples for salad. After a minute he said soberly: "It's more than my allowance. On top of what I eat I couldn't be worth that much."

"Could you wait until spring, Denny? Business will be better then."

I heard him catch his breath hard. "Sure, I can. Don't you worry about it."

He carried plates and silver to the table, keeping his face averted.

"Mom, is it all right with you if I go for a walk? I'm not hungry."

A few days later he wrote another business letter:

"Dear Mr. Richardson,

I guess our deal is off. I have the forty dollars but mother and father don't find it convenient just now to pay the $37.89 for the shed and the $3.19 a month for feed.

Yours respectfully,
Denny

P.S. I hope this does not inconvenience you any."

There is a golden, a perfect time for the fulfillment of a child's desires. Thwarted then, the glory fades, the hope will glow no longer.

One February afternoon I saw Denny, a package under his arm, starting down the road. I called, "Where are you going?"

"To the Heely stables. They will trade me a ride for my curry comb and brush."

That was more than a mile away. "Wait," I motioned, "I'll get the car."

"No," he said. "I'll walk."

I stood by the door to watch him. Such a slender little boy with his shirt tail out, walking down a desert road with the sun behind him. Such a thin little boy. But it seemed to me that he was casting quite a shadow.

The Judicial District

The first effort to establish law and order in this part of the desert was not too successful. The county sheriff appointed as deputy a trapper from the South. His qualifications: He owned a good assortment of firearms and was proud of his star. His idea of law enforcement combined the traditions of the Deep South and the Wild West. He was a member of the tar and feather party and his participation in that event resulted in his forced resignation.

In his place was appointed a gentle gentleman with the propitious name W. E. Ketcham.

There developed in the community an earnest desire to have our own judicial district with an elected justice of the peace and constable. A petition was drawn up and circulated. There were sixty-five signatures, enough to qualify. In February of 1930 the county established the Twentynine Palms Judicial District.

Samuel T. Bailey, a veteran with police experience, was appointed justice of the peace, and Guy Mattox, a husky Legionnaire, was made constable. These were temporary appointments pending an election. Later in the same year Louie Jacobs was elected justice of the peace and Gus Seely constable. Seely was a big-framed cattleman who settled near Coyote Well, east of Warren's Well. He was well liked, but resigned after two years saying that his work of enforcing the law was losing him too many friends. Jack Cones was made constable in his place. In 1935, Dave Poste was elected justice of the peace.

Louie Jacobs could preside at a trial with dignity and confidence and was gracious and kind in performing wedding ceremonies.

I recall the wedding of Alice, a girl of sixteen. She was

marrying a young mine foreman who was well respected and able to care for her. Because the bride was so young her friends were concerned that her wedding should have dignity and any beauty we could provide. It was held in a homestead cabin, loaned for the occasion. Bill Barnett and I were orchestra, playing on the porch, he with guitar and I with mandolin. Louie had arranged a small table like an altar, a fine white cloth, an open Bible, white candles.

Alice graciously wrote me afterward, thanking me for my part in making her wedding "so beautiful." It has been a good marriage.

I was called for the jury in what I believe was the second trial in the district. If my memory is uncertain, so was the evidence in the trial. It concerned an alleged hi-jack attempt at the Virginia Dale mine. We of the jury felt that the best parts of the story — as who shot a gun and why — were being carefully censored from our hearing. The chief witness for the prosecution was a man, not of our town, but well known as one to whom truth was of no consequence. The young lawyer, imported for the occasion, careful not to antagonize the jury by casting aspersions on this witness, said, "I do not wish to appear doubtful of the veracity of your fellow townsman, but may I call your attention to certain discrepancies in his testimony?"

When the jury retired — Bill Smith and Jim Byler were among them — they elected me as foreman. I said, "Before we begin deliberating, let us take a vote and see how we stand."

Ballots were passed and the vote was unanimous. We did not know what it was all about, but we knew right well that our "fellow townsman" would rather lie than tell the truth. We marched back into the courtroom, a garage rented for the day, and reported "Not Guilty."

The Virginia Dale Mine had a long and ruinous history of lawsuits and litigation. I doubt if any other case was ever settled so expeditiously. I hope we were right.

Dave Poste

Dave Poste was a rugged and enduring man. He had the good fortune to be married to Anna, who had humor, courage, red hair, and a sort of fire about her. Dave was elected justice of the peace for our Judicial District and served for many years. Anna and he also had the first telephone exchange in Twentynine Palms. This is how it came about.

Dave had worked most of his life, in various capacities, as a miner. He had been successful enough to accumulate capital. In 1923 he took a lease and bond on the Virginia Dale Mine from the Sigafus family and moved Anna to the New Dale. The remaining abandoned buildings stood open to the wind. The mine, too, was dilapidated. To explore its tunnels Dave sometimes crawled on his belly. He explored down to 300 feet; most of his work, however, was with the mill, getting it ready to operate.

In the evenings Anna and he often went to the old building which had been the post office and social hall when the mine was active. The billiard table and card table were still there. In the post office boxes were letters never called for. Anna and Dave played billiards by lantern light.

They believed in the mine. The ore was in finger-like stringers. It was Dave's theory and hope that at a lower level they would combine in a sizeable, workable, body of ore.

Part of the time he had a crew of sixteen men and a cook. Water was a problem. They had to bring it four miles and use a force pump to lift it up the hill. Dave knew he was running out of money. He had worked eighteen months and spent $40,000, but the mill was ready to operate. He started it, ran it four days, was stopped by a law suit.

They returned to the city, but they had not given up.

About 1930 they came back to the Dale. This time they had a large enough stake to get the mine working and paying. The money was in a savings bank in San Diego. The depression struck, the bank closed. They had nothing.

They left the mine and lived in a borrowed house near Twentynine Palms. Anna began to paint. She cut canvas from an old tent. She mixed paint using ground ore from mine tailings and turpentine and linseed oil. For brushes she combined the dog's hair with her own, bound to bamboo sticks. She painted the desert mountains with their own colors. With her courage as the catalyst she transmuted dirt and dross into the gold of beauty.

When the Works Progress Administration (W.P.A.) offered work Dave signed for labor. The office in our store was used by a clerk of the administration for registering men. I was on duty in the store that day. I saw the men going in, signing for pick and shovel work on the roads. Many were competent, skilled, but their skills were not needed. The offered jobs would provide bare necessities. They signed willingly, even with pride. Many of them had worked on the roads without thought of pay. Waiting on them as they emerged from the office and passed through the store, I blinked back tears and smiled, careful to be casual and friendly.

Dave and Anna were respected by everyone who knew them. It was in 1935 that Dave was elected justice of the peace. He had dignity, intelligence, and a strong sense of right and justice. The office paid a mere pittance, but he no longer needed to work with pick and shovel for the W.P.A. Anna managed.

There was at that time no telephone system in the community, only three long distance phones: at the Twentynine Palms Inn, at Donnell's Hotel, and at our store. We had come to know the representative of the California Water and Telephone Company who sometimes came from Redlands.

One day he came to see us. The Company wanted to establish a phone office and switchboard in Twentynine

Palms, but it must be handled with a small budget. Did we suppose it would be possible to get a man and his wife to serve the exchange, night and day, for $25 a month? We told him about the Postes. The phone man went immediately to see them.

The Postes then rented the one-room cabin near the store, the one known as the "teacher's cabin," for five dollars a month. They set up the switchboard and office at the front of the room, with a cot beside it. The remainder of the room was bedroom, living room and kitchen. Anna kept it neat, homelike and efficient.

When she had leisure Anna painted desert landscapes and made pottery from clay and the finely ground tailings of the mines. Her pottery was a delicate natural pink, not glazed but smoothed and polished by hand, distinctive.

Home phones were installed. Soon there were twelve of them, and leisure time vanished.

There was an assurance, especially when there was an emergency or sickness, in hearing the voice of Anna or Dave on the telephone. Both the trivial and the tragic were handled in that office with efficiency and compassion.

It was to this office that Bill Keys came one day. "Judge Poste," he said, "I have shot a man."

"Is he dead?"

"I think so. I watched him for about twenty minutes and he did not move."

Dave said quietly, "Anna, will you please take the switchboard? Call Constable Cones."

Dave then called Sheriff Shay and arranged for him to meet Keys and Jack Cones at the scene of the shooting.

After they had left the office Dave said quietly, "Anna, you may go on with your painting. I'll take the phone again."

The Postes bought the cabin and enlarged it. When the switchboard became so busy that another operator was needed they hired Blanche. She happily carried on the Postes' custom of being neighborly and helpful.

I once called about one o'clock and gave Bill Hatch's

Jack Cones. "Men who knew him best said he was without fear."

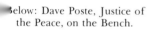

Below: Dave Poste, Justice of the Peace, on the Bench.

number. "But Helen," said the operator, "don't you know that Bill Hatch usually takes a nap after lunch? Oh well — it is only one o'clock. Since it is you — he may not mind."

If a call was of importance and the number did not answer, Anna and Blanche would try to figure out where that person might be and call another number. In an emergency Dave would get in his car and travel miles to deliver a message.

Long distance operators must have been astonished at the service in Twentynine Palms. A lady in Vermont once urgently called Martha Ann Smith, who had only recently come to town and was living in the motel near the phone office. Blanche also lived in that motel and she had just come on duty. Walking to work she had noticed a delectable fragrance as she passed a certain door. When Martha Ann did not answer the phone, the Vermont operator asked, "Can she be reached at another number?"

"No," said Blanche, "but I am sure she won't be away long, because she has an apple pie in the oven."

Dave's dual role occasioned some interesting moments. His voice was deep and had a note of authority even in taking a number. One day he received a long distance call from a man who had a problem and was looking for trouble. He was demanding and hostile. Finally he ordered:

"Well then — get me the justice of the peace."

Dave's voice went one note lower. "This is the Justice of the Peace."

The stranger hung up.

As time passed and the population grew, a larger exchange was needed. David and Anna relinquished the home office. They were missed. Service was never the same again.

Dave was re-elected as "Judge" for term after term. When he retired in 1951 the community gave a banquet to honor him.

Dave had come to the desert to mine for gold. He found it in the affection and esteem of the frontier community he served.

Jack Cones

Orville Jackson Cones — Jack — "The Flying Constable" was appointed Constable of the Twentynine Palms Judicial District in 1932. Afterwards he was reelected five times. He was of medium height, strongly built, and heavy. He weighed two hundred fifty pounds. His face was round and usually pleasant. He was thirty-five years old, and he had lived a lot.

The Twentynine Palms Judicial District is about forty miles wide and seventy miles long, and the constable was on duty twenty-four hours a day. In the beginning he was paid $25.00 a month. He might be busy day and night, or there might be no calls for a week.

He found time to be a Scout Master, and he worked with every constructive enterprise in the village. Perhaps he is most gratefully remembered as a volunteer driver of the community ambulance. For many years there was no doctor and no hospital within fifty miles. Often a life depended on the community ambulance. Driving it was not part of Jack's duty. He was just ready any time he was needed.

Clara, his wife, often rode with the patient, giving such comfort as she could. Sometimes people were deathly ill; sometimes delirious and mean. Sometimes it was terribly hot and they smelled bad. They made many trips to San Bernardino, the county seat, and farther.

In their home, Clara also had a part. There was no jail, no place of detention. Jack had a problem with drunks, because if he took them to the county jail in San Bernardino, nearly one hundred miles distant, they could be sober by the time he got there. And if a man was locked up over night, then the poor fellow had to find a way home the next day. So Jack usually stayed overnight to bring him back again. Very often Jack just took the drunks home and Clara helped sober them. People who were sick and destitute and needed a friend rather than more trouble might be taken to the Cones' house.

Jack knew a great deal about trouble. His mother had died when he was very young, and as a child he had been shifted from place to place where he was not always welcome and not often happy. Then his father remarried. The stepmother had a piano, and when no one was around Jack learned to pick out tunes. He proudly played one for his father. His father gave him a licking and threatened worse if he ever caught him doing such a sissy thing again. (The first luxury Jack bought for himself and Clara, when his salary was raised, was a piano. It seemed a strange thing for him to do.)

At fourteen he left home and worked on cattle ranches. At twenty he served with the Texas National Guard on the Mexican Border; the next year he enlisted in the United States Army and was sent to France. In France and Belgium he was General Pershing's personal motorcycle dispatch rider. He was severely wounded in the foot and leg. Ever after he walked with a slight limp and the disability was painful for an active man who was so heavy.

He told me this story: while he was in bed, unable to walk, he was confined in a ward on the second story of a hospital near the front. There was a bombing raid. He said, "I was heavy even then but my nurse somehow got me up across her hip and carried me down two flights to the bomb shelter in the basement." He hesitated, then added shyly, "Every year I send her roses."

When Jack came home from the war he went to the country where he had lived, hired a horse, and rode out to the house where he had felt most at home. There were lights in the house and he rode around it, but he was not sure that every one in that house would be glad to see him back. So he just rode around again, in the dark, and finally he went back to the livery stable.

A few years later Jack and Clara met in Long Beach.

Thus began a companionship, then a marriage, and a sharing of life and work from which the desert community benefited. Clara was a deeply religious person. She expressed her faith in tolerance and kindness. Her quiet sense of humor helped her through trying situations. They homesteaded in Twentynine Palms in 1928.

Men who knew Jack best said he was without fear. He could handle rowdy toughs, disarm a maniac, go up to a murderer and take his gun away from him. Jack himself had not wanted to carry a gun; he did so only after the sheriff ordered it. And he would not put handcuffs on a man even though he had to drive him, alone, all the way to San Bernardino. He had a steady quiet assurance that commanded respect. If he felt no fear it was because he was self forgetful and danger was part of his job.

He built the first air strip in Twentynine Palms and opened it to the public. He learned to fly and was owner of a Piper Cub. To a man who weighed two hundred and fifty pounds and had a lame foot, a man who dealt with trouble all day, it must have been a joy to fly. But he made it a service to the community. He became known, even famous, as "The Flying Constable."

For years he used the plane at his own expense. With it he could really cover his big district. He could check back roads for motorists in trouble, look for evidence of vandalism at the closed mines, watch the humble cabins for signals of distress. It gave remote and lonely people a sense of security to see him flying over.

He found runaway horses. Once, believe it or not, he located a piece of pavement that had been stolen and moved. More than once he landed near a woman motorist who was stalled in the sand, helped her to get out, then flew off again. More important, he was able to find and then lead to the capture of an escaped mental patient.

There is often a good deal of the boy left in a man who has had to grow up too soon. This was true of Jack. When the Judicial District became too much of a responsibility for one man, the county sheriff sent young deputies to aid in patrol and law enforcement. Jack at first resented them. They were trained and better educated than he; perhaps they were amused at the way he wrote up reports for the office record. But they soon learned to respect and admire him.

One day a woman who was walking across the desert, not far from the village center, was killed by a shot from a small house on the crest of a hill. The killer went into this house and did not reappear. Extra deputies, from headquarters, surrounded the place, crouching behind greasewood bushes. They used a loud speaker to order the suspect to come out and surrender. There was no reply. They were considering rushing the house, or using tear gas, when Jack arrived. He knew the man inside. To the deputies he said, "Wait." He walked up the hill, knocked at the door, and went in.

"Lloyd," he said, "give me your gun."

Jack was killed in an airplane crash in 1960. He was not far aloft; it is supposed that he suffered a heart attack.

His funeral was held in the small white church Clara loved. The deputies marched in, uniformed, two abreast, and filled the front benches.

The community was moved with grief. There was the wish to do something to commemorate Jack, to express love and esteem. Because I was at hand in the store, people began sending or giving me money. A committee was formed to handle the fund. One of the first contributions came from a man who, as a boy of twelve, had shot the windows of a vacant building with a new air rifle. Jack had returned the rifle to him when he was a year older. The man he had arrested for murder had served his term in prison. He sent a twenty dollar bill and wrote, "Jack and Clara always made me welcome in their home."

I have not tried to write of Jack as a hero. He did heroic things but to him they were just part of his job. It was his humaneness, the way he did his job, that made him loved. It was the things he did day by day that were above and beyond the call of duty.

The committee discussed whether we should use the words, "Beloved Flying Constable," on the plaque we designed. But they decided that the fact there is a plaque shows that he was loved.

The artist, working from photographs, caught something of the sadness and kindness in Jack's face. In the corner he put a Piper Cub, taking off. It is a symbol of his continuing life and influence. It can be seen in the hall of the County building on Adobe Road in Twentynine Palms:

Jack Cones Flying Constable
Guardian of the Peace
Friend of Man

V. Day's Work

"Neighbors Lend a Hand"
Adobe Road
Greasewood, Sage and Sand
The General Store

"Neighbors Lend a Hand"

When there was water in our well we began to build a house. We had drawn our own plans, four rooms with a long screen porch across the back. The front of the house was at right angles to the front of the store, and I carefully figured the space so that from my kitchen sink I could look through a window and by counting cars parked by the store know whether I was needed to help.

Frank worked with local carpenters. One old man, when he was hired, boasted: "I'm one of the very few left who knows how to cut them ovals for your outhouse." This was a talent not required for we were to have the luxury of indoor plumbing. He assured Frank that he had learned to hang doors and windows from a Sears Roebuck Catalog. Mr. Hockett, who was also helping with the water tank, often stated: "I don't believe in working myself out of a job." But he was steady.

Lumber was being hauled in by Jim Hill, a miner, an ex-prize fighter and blacksmith, whose ancient Pope truck would break down on nearly every trip. He was determined to complete the job. He carried along his blacksmith tools, and when the truck broke down he set up his anvil by the side of the road and made repairs. He was often away overnight and his frail wife, Iva, was left alone. She was a trained nurse and she had used her skills generously in the rough country. She did not complain of hardships, but when a splinter group from the Tar and Feather party called upon her, naming themselves, "The Purple Burros" and making veiled threats, she was terrified. This was too much for her husband Jim. Trips for lumber were halted while he did some threatening of his own.

When the floor was laid Frank came to me. I was on duty in the store while he worked on the building. He tore off a piece of wrapping paper and spread it on the counter. He said, "We are about to begin framing. How do you want the doors and windows spaced? I'll wait on people. Draw it out."

A few days later he called me to the job. "What pitch shall we make the roof?" Two men held up timbers. "No," I said. "Try higher. There, that is good." And I went back to our boys and the customers.

We painted the house white with a green trim and built a stone fireplace on one end. And then we found that its simplicity of line reminded us of something. In the Mojave Desert we had built a Cape Cod cottage. We lived in it and enjoyed it for eighteen years.

Cuttings from Bill Smith's athol trees took root around our yard. Athol trees are the homesteader's friend. They grow from cuttings given by a neighbor and they have, therefore, a genealogy tracing back to a miner who wanted shade beside his cabin, or a cattleman with a tank for his herd, and from one homesteader to another. Once they have rooted athols will live without care and wait for the man who has to go to town to earn enough to carry him through another season. The trees will welcome him with green when he returns. They need not be taller than a child when he can hear the wind in them at night. And to anyone who grew up as I had within hearing of pine trees and the sea, the sound of wind in even a very small tree is a marvelously comforting thing. When I could hear the wind in our trees I no longer felt myself an exile.

With the kitchen and dining room out of the store there was another wall for shelves. Frank added to the back of the eighteen foot garage and made a storage shed at the side with an office behind it.

Boxes of dynamite for the miners were kept in that office. A stack of four or five cases made a comfortable seat. The miners felt at home there when they came in to consult about credit for their supplies. They would bring in samples of their richest gold ore and these gradually accumulated in a pile in the corner. "Lookit this, Mr. Bagley. I think it may go ninety dollars to the ton."

A man with a badly cut hand was given first aid in that office by Art Krushat, who had learned his skill in the Navy. All sorts of problems were threshed out there — including our own perpetual struggle with accounts receivable and accounts payable.

Such privacy was also a convenience to irate customers. One day Jim Byler, glowering, urgently motioned Frank into the office and shut the door. He stood across the work table, leaning forward with his big fists on the table. He was taut and quivering with anger.

"Say," he demanded, "did you tell Bud that I am crazy?"

Frank leaned forward, too, facing him squarely. "I told him," he stated, "that you are AWOL from a psychopathic ward; that you are a good guy and generous to a fault; that you would give a man the shirt off your back; but that you can't be depended on from day to day. Now — is that the truth — or isn't it?"

Jim straightened up and took two strides to the door. "It's true," he said, and slammed the office door behind him.

The first fixture we bought for the grocery store, aside from carpenter-made shelves and counters, was a bulk goods case. This was a case with glass partitions, designed for storage and display. We used it for beans, all kinds of beans. It had cost fifty dollars and we were very proud of it. This stood near the door to the office with our second-hand cash register on top and cubbyholes for the mail behind it.

At the back of the room, between the shelves for ammunition and the hard-toed shoes, we made room for the books of the county library. It was a fine service of the county library, begun by Miss Caroline Waters, to establish a small branch in a store or public place in nearly every settlement of mountain or desert in the huge county of San Bernardino.

During the days in Pasadena, when I was struggling with myself over the decision to move to the desert, I looked up

at the carved motto above the door of the Pasadena City
Library. It read:

"Be made whole by books, as by wide spaces and the
stars."

I thought, "Wide spaces and the stars I will certainly
have and I can get the books." Now — horizons had no
bounds.

On the shelves beside the ammunition we placed household drugs and first-aid supplies. It was sixty miles to a
drug store and most of the time there was no doctor nearer.

A few kegs of nails were under a shelf. Coleman lanterns, cans for kerosene, canvas water bags swung from the
rafters. Sometimes when the truck came in we said to each
other, "We've done it now. We can't possibly put this stuff
away."

I was never comfortable with gasoline appliances, although we used them for years. I once demonstrated a
gasoline iron for a customer, set the top of the counter
afire, but sold the iron. At the time, I hopefully thought
that my salesmanship was improving, but probably she was
sorry for me.

The cubbyholes behind the bean case represented progress. Mail was no longer brought in by the trucker. A post
office and mail route had been established in the spring of
1928. The post office department required as a condition
for establishing the route that the mail should be driven for
two months without cost to the department. Mr. Edward
Bixby had performed this service; his gas and oil were furnished by others in the community.

Frank had written to the authorities asking to be appointed postmaster. The Inn, however, was chosen for the
post office, and Miss Frances Roberts was made postmistress. For many of our customers this meant extra driving
and for those who requested it, Frank brought their mail
over with his own. In time, Miss Roberts left the Inn and
the new manager, a man of very different type, resented
having miners and homesteaders, especially men in rough

clothing or bib overalls, waiting for mail around his "resort hotel." There may have been other problems too.

One day Frank received an official letter from the post office department which said, in effect though with many more words, "If you still want the post office, go and get it."

He drove over in his pickup truck. The section of screen with the mail boxes and the delivery window was lying face downward on the floor. Letters were sticking up in the boxes or scattered about. The manager, who had been acting postmaster, was nowhere around. Frank gathered up the mail, the partition with the boxes, and all the books on official regulations he could find, and brought them back with him. In a few hours the small building which had been our tent-house sleeping room, then our warehouse, was equipped with mail boxes, a general delivery window, and proudly bore a sign "29 Palms Post Office." (Later, by order of the Department, the name was changed to its present form, Twentynine Palms, to avoid confusion in addresses.)

Having Frank for postmaster meant that anyone could get service day or night, since it was only a step to our house.

A car shelter at the side of the post office building was closed in and made a restaurant which could seat as many as six customers at a time, two at a table by a window and four at the counter. The food was good and daintily served. It was operated by Hilda and Jim Graham.

John had his first job there. For cranking a freezer of ice cream he was paid one hamburger.

The success of the tiny cafe made it necessary to enlarge. Frank agreed to furnish lumber if Jim would do the work. With Les Earenfight to help him, Jim tore down the east wall while Hilda was serving breakfast. The customers were delighted — they stayed to watch. The wall was framed in and by evening the men were laying the floor while Hilda stood in a corner and cooked. There were fifteen for dinner. The width of the building had been doubled to eighteen feet.

Tom Martin was a mechanic but when he first came to

the desert he had to take any job available. One afternoon, coming from work, he stopped at the store to get his mail. He found Frank down on the floor, the parts of his Fairbanks Morse light plant laid out around him. Frank looked up, saw Tom watching him — grinning. He got up from the floor and said,

"Fix it."

The next year Tom Martin had a garage. In a village with rough roads, old cars, and secondhand machinery in most installations, no enterprise could have been more welcome. Tom would work with skill and good conscience on anything from a boy's roller skate to a Cadillac.

People began to call our homestead "Bagley's Center."

There was another store in the village. Clovis and Mary Benito had contracted to carry the mail from Whitewater to Twentynine Palms, serving a star route along the way. At first there were fifteen boxes on the route. Clovis put up a building at the corner of Sullivan and Adobe Roads; Mary drove the mail route and brought merchandise and groceries for their store. Produce was a problem because the front of their market was open and burros nibbled the lettuce. After he had made an adequate door, Clovis added a gas pump and a garage. Mary Benito comments,

"You had to do more than one thing."

Their first contract for the mail route was $1,500 a year for three trips a week. Later this was increased for six trips. Assisted by her sons Mary drove more than five years, using secondhand Cadillacs for trucks and "never missed a trip."

The depression hit Twentynine Palms in 1931. Most of us were so poor anyway that it was a year or more before before the national situation was felt. The cubbyholes behind the bean case, where we had once held mail for people, were now used for sales books for charge accounts. Frank proved up on his land in time to mortgage it.

Art Krushat had joined us during those difficult days. A Navy veteran, once a submarine man, he had worked in a general store in Wisconsin as a boy. We took on a terminolgy strange in so dry a land. The meat case became a locker, we swabbed the deck, and the truck came to port alongside the dock. Art insisted that we let him go to town to buy our supplies and we bought a station wagon for that purpose. He would leave at three o'clock in the morning, drive to Riverside and San Bernardino, get back at three in the afternoon and work until closing time. It was his idea of the way a store should be run.

The chief problem of our truckers was always "special orders." Art was patient and serious about them. A special order might be anything not available in Twentynine Palms — or even something we carried, "but cheaper at Sears." A birthday card "For Sister," grey shoelaces, baled hay, dynamite. And woe to us and all our works if there were no grey shoelaces to be found.

We once put this ad in the *Desert Outpost*, the first weekly news sheet:

"Yes, we are not an agent for Sears Roebuck or Montgomery Ward."

A customer bawled Frank out for it. The man had found it convenient to have our trucker buy for him, thus saving postage, charging the cost to his account and paying at his leisure.

Because the services were needed Frank began to write fire insurance and acquired a notary's license. As a notary he took final proofs for the Land Office and they often sent to him people who were looking for homestead sites. Much of his time was spent in just answering questions. In 1934 he became wholesale distributor for the Standard Oil Company; and so it came about that he forgot such details as the price of cheese and left the management of the store more to me and to Art.

There is an old story, delightful to remember just now, of Frank trying to sell a customer a porterhouse steak for stew meat. The man refused it because there was too much bone. Once when Frank was left alone in the store an old man came in with a complaint. He said, "That sugar looked nice and clean, but I was boiling it for syrup and it got full of cobwebs." Since Frank had never heard of testing boiling syrup to see if it would spin a thread, he apologized and gave another sack.

Besides the bulletin board at our homestead store, the first news medium for this area was the American Legion Foundation's *The Outpost, The Valley Newspaper,* a mimeographed sheet about 8 x 10 inches. With E. H. Abernethy as editor, it carried a surprising amount of news, mining and personal as well as Legion activities. It was first printed in June 1932, when Twentynine Palms was hardly a village, and continued into its third volume. For about a year most of the news was disseminated by word of mouth.

Then in the spring of 1935, Bill Underhill, who had homesteaded in 1928, began publishing *The Desert Trail.* He was a man of great energy and zest, and he ventured boldly. He started out using equipment discarded by other printers, and composing his news stories on a linotype machine. As yet there was no phone, so all news gathering must be done in person. He was a familiar figure, standing with the crowd waiting for mail, noting on a bit of pad any newsworthy item he might learn. More than once all his material was blown away by a sudden storm. When he began to take subscriptions he offered a three month trial for fifty cents — a bargain if one could believe the paper would survive that long.

Writing stories on a linotype does not conduce to referring to a dictionary. "Gentle readers" took delight in watching for goofs. Once in a lead story about the wedding of two esteemed citizens, a front page double column announced:

"Marriage Consummated
United in Matrimony before an Arizona Justice."

Later Underhill married Prudence Mason who owned a typewriter. The *Desert Trail* prospered — but there were no more goofs. Through the years Bill and Prudence also provided for the town a roller rink, an indoor theater and two outdoor theaters.

Mrs. Nellie Coffman of Palm Springs came to call on me. She had been the pioneer spirit of her town, loved and honored for her contributions to the community, and she was the builder and owner of the beautiful Desert Inn. She came to inquire how it was that Twentynine Palms had a high school when Palm Springs did not. I told her the story as I have related it in the chapter on the school.

She was cordial and friendly; I wanted to know her better. The day was hot and we had no air conditioning. How could I entertain her?

Frank and I took her to Bill Smith's place. The athol trees, where we used to let the water run while we bathed, had grown to great size. Bill had made a picnic ground beneath them, tables and chairs for anyone who wished to rest in their shade. He had an ice cream shop, wooden stools along a counter, his homemade ice cream was a treat.

Nellie Coffman of the Desert Inn perched happily on a square topped stool, and with Bill and Thelma exchanged reminiscences of frontier days. One of her stories I remember. Her father had protested her plan to invest in desert wasteland. He had said,

"Palm Springs is nothing but a sand pile."

She had replied, "Yes — but it is the sand pile in the back yard of Los Angeles."

By 1936, Twentynine Palms was more than a village — it was two or three of them. The Four Corners was developing. There were business places too numerous to mention.

The sides of our store were bulging. On cold evenings people would wait for mail in the store. It was due about six o'clock. The room would be so crowded that it was almost impossible to serve anyone. There was a small potbellied stove at the far end which became a social center. As soon as the first warm days of March came Art would take it down. In April Frank would set it up again.

We began to feel embarrassed because our four-room house was larger than our store.

Adobe Road

Adobe Road? Why the name? It was the main crossroad in Twentynine Palms, the most traveled and the worst. It ran north to the dry lake, south to cross the Twentynine Palms Highway and on to Base Line. For three miles north of the Two Mile Road it ran through sand dunes and blowsand. At the northern end there was a homestead and a house to nearly every quarter section, "the congested area." Many people lived there and for years they struggled with that road. After every rain someone would scrape it. It would appear smooth and passable but the surface would wear to ruts and then to sand again. Even experienced drivers might get stuck in that road. But that was the way to travel to get to Smith's Ranch, to the post office in Bagley's Center, and to the school.

The homesteaders brought the white salts from the dry lake and spread them; they just worked into the sand.

The group of people who lived on Indian Trail and on Valle Vista Road were the most determined and cooperative. They had formed a club, "The Valle de las Vistas Club."

The name of the club was significant of their spirit. We used to say, "Every homesteader thinks he has the most beautiful view in the valley." Many of us had chosen the hills, but those who lived in the valley looked toward mountains that rimmed the long basin, the bare mountains, changing color from cool gray of morning to rosy tints of evening, and loved all they saw. They joined in friendship and in willingness to work together.

Men used their trucks and hauled adobe from the dry lake. With shovels and drags they spread it on the sandy road. Women and children rode on the drags to give them

weight and cars were driven back and forth to pack the surface. And for a time there was a surface. We proudly called
it Adobe Road. Then it rained. The adobe was mud. Cars
bogged down and when they were dug out the hole that was
left became impassable.

The Valle de las Vistas Club met again. That road must
be paved. Burl Stonecipher and my Frank were appointed
as "The Twentynine Palms Road Oiling Committee." They
had already talked to those county men responsible for the
roads, Howard Way, the Highway Commissioner, and
Ralph Motherspaw who was in charge of construction and
maintenance. They had been told that it would cost about
$700 a mile just to buy oil, and that the county could not
allocate any more money to the district. But they went to
Motherspaw again. "If the people of the community can
raise the money for three miles of oil will the county use its
equipment to spread it?" they asked.

Ralph Motherspaw said amicably, "Oh sure."

He knew the homesteaders of our neighborhood, or
thought he did. They had no money. Raise $2,000? Too
bad. That stretch of road really was a mess.

Bagley the grocer? Everyone knew he was in debt up to
his ears with that new store building. Burl Stonecipher? Did
he have a steady job?

It was true that they had no money, but they were not
poor.

Burl and Frank went to Mr. Morrison of the Bank of
Beaumont. "If the homesteaders would mortgage their land
for just a nominal sum, say five dollars an acre, would the
bank take their notes as security and let them have the
money to buy oil for this road?"

Mr. Morrison said, "I think we can arrange it."

Burl and Frank reported to the club. The members
went to work to contribute and to spread news of the effort.
There were seventy contributors on the final list. A few
gifts, from $1 to $10, were from friends who gave just to
help, but the more substantial sums were from those who
used the road.

A small part of these donations were paid in cash, but the larger amounts and some for only $25 were given as notes secured by mortgages. A letter to the Bank of Beaumont, dated July 21, 1937, read:

"Gentlemen:
I am enclosing ten grant deeds and twelve quit claim deeds for corresponding land to be filed with the Bagley and Stonecipher notes held by you. The grant deeds are all recorded."

These were only part of the mortgages on land at five dollars an acre. There were even a few chattel mortgages.

The homesteaders were so pleased with their accomplishment that they expected the oil and the county equipment to arrive the next afternoon. But days passed, a week, three weeks. Then one morning,

"Glory be," exclaimed Frank. "They are oiling the road."

In a few days there was a smooth paved road.

And then we heard that Ralph Motherspaw had died. We felt that we had lost a friend. But we did not know how good a friend. A month later another county employee told Frank this story.

When Motherspaw received the check and appeared before the Board of Supervisors with the proposition for oiling the road they said,

"No. Not under any circumstances. No."

Ralph had tried for a week to change the board's attitude. Finally he appeared again at their next meeting. He said:

"Gentlemen, I admit I had no idea those people could raise that much money. I know what it meant for them to do it. But I gave my word. I'm sorry. But you will either oil that road or get another highway foreman to take my place . . ."

The supervisors thought that over for another week, and then they said, "Go ahead."

Greasewood, Sage and Sand

Sometime in the early thirties an old man in a homemade camper drove to our store, parked, and went in to Frank. He spread a brochure with a map on the counter and asked to be directed to a lot he had already bought. On the map it appeared that the lot was only a block or two from the "City Hall" and quite near Donnell's Mission Inn. Actually it was a mile or two distant in undeveloped land, just short of nowhere. Frank pointed out the approximate location. The old man would not even go to see it.

He left his camper parked by the store for several days, sat on the stone benches talking and observing. Before he left he took me aside.

He said, "Do you see them mountains?" He pointed to the Sheep Holes.

"Yes."

He motioned to the Little San Bernardinos. "Do you see them mountains?"

"Yes."

His gesture included the far off mountains to the west. "Do you see them?"

"Yes."

"Everything between them mountains is real estate." He then got into his truck and drove away.

It was typical of California during those years that land was sold undeveloped and often misrepresented, sold by high presssure salesmen to people who had not seen it. One such salesman, when Frank protested his methods, replied, "A person who buys desert land is just a sucker anyway."

To homesteaders who loved the wide space and freedom of the desert, this was abhorrent. The idea of sixty-foot lots was revolting. But not everyone who wanted to live in the desert could have a big piece of land and his own well. To have utilities there must be planning, and the State of California tightened its regulations on the sale of land.

Ole Hanson, who had once been Mayor of Seattle and had recently promoted the city of San Clemente, came to Twentynine Palms and really liked it. In 1934 he opened a subdivision on the hill slope south of the Oasis. Soon the Southwest Subdividers built an office at the Four Corners. Hanson's organization in the Los Angeles district would send out caravans to see his tract. They had to pass the Southwest office and sometimes they went no further. Another company started up about two miles west in the Smoke Tree area. "Go west, young man, go west" — and get them first.

We needed a larger store, and after much indecision and planning we decided to build on the corner of our own homestead and to develop a small shopping center. In order to do this and to sell lots it was necessary to subdivide. We filed for Tract 2530 on the corner of Two Mile Road and Adobe Road in July of '36.

Frank furnished water to the lots in this location and later supplied water to another tract of acreage plots. The charge for water was at first two dollars a month. The responsibility of operating these services was a strain and a hazard.

Sara and Leonard Wikoff, in 1937, started their electric light plant at the Four Corners. Their neighbors turned out to pour the cement block for the twenty-five horsepower Fairbanks Morse generator which was their first machine. Lack of capital and inadequate equipment made this courageous undertaking a strain for the Wikoffs too. One day when the power had been shut off for several hours, Leonard confided to me that he had attacked his own plant with an iron bar. He said it made him feel much better.

When the power was available, Frank subdivided two strips of lots along the east and south boundaries of our homestead, on Adobe Road and on Two Mile Road.

After a few years we were able to sell the water system to

Gene Abell and the electrical lines to Wikoff. This was a
great relief. Anyone who is resentful of public utilities
should try having his own.

When the plan for our shopping center had been filed
and accepted we engaged an architect. We had inherited
ten thousand dollars and to us it seemed an enormous sum.
This time we did not want our building to turn out looking
like a garage or a Cape Cod cottage. We wanted it to be
beautiful, a part of the desert. We determined the location
by facing it toward the Sheep Hole Mountains, our most
glorious view.

The man we asked to draw our plans was a distinguished architect, one who designed churches and public
buildings. We would never have presumed to approach him
had he not been our friend. Because of our friendship, and
his own kindness, he agreed to draw our elevation and floor
plan for a fee which was probably less than his expenses. He
came out to see us and we sat together poring over a book
of California Colonial buildings. He understood how we
felt, our wish for beauty after nine years in a garage. In a
picture of a Monterey adobe we found a plan which would
use and enhance the sloping contour of our land. There
were to be three levels: a room for the post office at the
higher level, with our offices back of it, then ninety feet of
frontage for the market, and at the lowest level a service
station with a long canopy to extend the lines.

When he sent the elevation of the building, drawn as
architects draw, with a suggestion of color and a few palm
trees added, Frank and I were thrilled. It was beautiful and
it suited the land. Certainly it did not suggest anything from
Cape Cod or a garage. That it did not look like a grocery
store either did not immediately concern us. There was a
tile roof, iron grills on the windows, heavy pillars of adzed
wood, and inside, massive beams supporting an open ceiling
for the main room of the market.

I regret that I can not disclose the name of this excellent
architect, but the reason will appear.

We lost no time taking this plan to Walter Berg, the

master builder and contractor of the community. When he submitted his estimate we were shocked and sick. I do not remember the figure, but it was twice what we could afford. We just laid the plan aside. There were some benches of stone slabs and some poplar trees in front of our garage building; we tried to think that they were beautiful.

After a few weeks, however, Walt came to us. "When do I start?" he asked.

We told him that we could not bring ourselves to go back to something like a cracker box, but the building designed for us was beyond our means.

"Well — " said Walt. "Let me make a few changes and I can build for about four dollars a square foot."

We did, and he did. The roof was shingle, the porch had a concrete floor, the pillars were sturdy but not adzed; the only wrought iron was the rail for the three steps which led from the market to the office and post office on the higher level. We did regret giving up the canopy above the service station. Even we could see the value of that extended line. Leaving the gas pumps in the open did, however, make them more noticeable.

We still loved the long, earth-clinging line; we still thought it beautiful. We put benches on the porch so that people could rest and visit and enjoy the view.

When our friend the architect came to see us, we were proud. He looked at the building for five short minutes and he turned white.

"Frank," he said, "don't you ever dare to use my name in connection with this building in any way whatever."

So I have not.

Before the shelves were in we celebrated with a dance — a store-warming dance. The crowd, the flowers, the good wishes, warmed our hearts as well.

In the room which was to be the post office we set up tables for card games. Refreshments were served in the outer office; people danced on the main floor. We hoped that when they climbed the three steps to find coffee and punch they would notice the wrought iron hand rails.

The orchestra was Ruth Nichols at the piano, our son John with a guitar, and Les Cross (the finish carpenter) with his saw. The rhythm was wonderful.

We moved in on New Year's Day, 1937. And we realized at once that the place was too small.

We owed everyone. Walt Berg knew only one way to build, substantially and well. And he had done a good job in keeping costs low. But we had not figured enough for gas pumps and service station equipment, or for the expense of extending our own water and electric power lines to the new building. There was already a chattel mortgage, and contracts to pay off. Humbly we went to the Bank of Beaumont to arrange a mortgage loan. The bank manager, Mr. Morrison, had been good to us and was used to our ways. The first time we ever submitted a financial statement to him he had remarked with a wry smile, "I never before saw 'bad debts' listed as an asset." Our previous loans had been for amounts like five hundred dollars. This time we needed three thousand.

He listened to us kindly in his private office. Then he said, "There is about to be a director's meeting. Wait here and I will submit your application."

The directors met in a room at the other end of the small bank. The rooms were partitioned but the ceiling was open. We could hear quite well because it was after hours and no one else was working. I heard a woman's voice:

"I don't want any part of it. I understand they are dead beats."

My heart was a stone.

Then Mr. Morrison's voice, very quiet, "They have just spent ten thousand dollars on a new building. Now they want to mortgage it to pay their debts. That is not being a dead beat."

We got the loan.

A few years later Frank served on the Board of Directors for the Bank of Beaumont. It gave him special pleasure.

The shopping center developed gradually, Hilda and

James Graham bought the lot just south of our store and built a new cafe. The elevation for this had been designed by the same architect who designed our building. James did most of the work himself and the structure was unique and attractive. There was a fireplace in the dining room and when friends gathered there for Sunday evening dinner we felt that we belonged to cafe society.

This later served as "The Artist's Workshop." Its design has never been changed and it is the only business building of that period in the town to retain its original charm and distinction.

Next to the cafe was a dress shop owned by Mr. and Mrs. Dan Leahy. A year or two later Phil Zimmers, a local architect, constructed a building which was used for doctor's offices and shops. Other buildings followed.

We had named this center Supply Place in the days when mining was a principal industry. We were persuaded by the new business people to call it "The Plaza" and it is so known today.

A later homesteader once said to us, "Weren't you lucky to get your store right in the middle of everything!"

General Store

THE WALL STREET JOURNAL — February 17, 1940
"PEPPER and SALT"
General Store

Out on the Colorado desert, which derives its name from the river and not from the state, Frank Bagley runs the general store, the focal point for the needs of a hundred odd miles of desert country. The store, located at Twentynine Palms, California, is more than a store — it is an institution of many years standing. Its many functions include banking and grub-staking miners. His family apparently includes some poetic talent, and the difficulties of running a general store are outlined in the poem which he paid for as an advertisement in the local *Desert Trail*.

There is something about a general store
(Sometimes it's less, sometimes it's more)
      You may find a shovel, you may find a hat,
      They'll be out of this but have plenty of that.

You can buy a thimble or a frying pan,
A birthday card or a gasoline can,
      Baby ribbon or dynamite,
      A hair net or a carbide light.

Camembert cheese or a box of snuff,
(They'll order more if there's not enough).
      Sliced bologna or free advice,
      Hard toe shoes or a pound of rice.

A place to sit and hear the news,
Drink soda pop and air your views,
      A corner for lovers who want to hold hands,
      Free directions to homestead lands.

Oh, you may find a shovel, you may find a hat,
They're out of this but have plenty of that;
   Sometimes it's less, sometimes it's more,
   But there's something about a general store.

I had written this doggerel, "General Store," on a Sunday afternoon at home, and included it in our Christmas ad. Alan had suggested another verse:

"Credit up to a hundred
   And then
You get a new book
   And start over again."

It seemed the better part of discretion to omit this.

The printer set my verse in very small type to leave space for prices of turkeys and such. No one mentioned it. I could not tell whether it had been read. But a tourist in town, a lady who was married to an editor of the *Wall Street Journal*, cut it out and sent it to her husband. He used it in the brief column, "Pepper and Salt." Some friend mailed a copy back to us.

I include it here because I can not better describe the store as it was in the late thirties. The woman who wrote the note for the *Wall Street Journal* had been discerning. It was not a very good store but it was an institution of sorts.

She spoke of banking. The nearest bank was in Banning and Frank undertook to cash checks, even pay rolls for the mines. This was generally known. But people sometimes brought to the store small sums and left them as deposits rather than carry cash.

The first such incident occurred at the time when banks were closing all over the country. Walter Ketcham brought in fifty dollars and asked that we keep it as a credit balance. He explained, "If I send this to my bank and it closes I will have nothing. If I leave it here and the store goes broke I can come in and get some cans."

On that not too optimistic expression of confidence we accepted the money.

More than once a man entrusting us with his cash would refuse to take the receipt we handed him. "No, I might lose it. Just keep it here."

Phil Sullivan, one of the early homesteaders and miners, sold land at the "Four Corners." His wife, a quiet woman who had shared his hardships through long years, came to the store and asked to speak to Frank in his office.

"Mr. Bagley," she said, "I have all this money now, and I am going to visit my home in Texas. The money I will need I have sewed in my dress, but this is too much. I want to leave it with you."

It was less than one thousand dollars, but no doubt it was more than she had ever before had for herself. Frank was touched by her confidence.

"You might need this when you are traveling," he said. "I'll write you my check. If you take this to a bank where you are staying in Texas they won't cash it for you right away, but they will collect the money and give it to you."

He wrote out his check and handed it to her. She accepted it gravely, read it carefully. She pushed it back across the table. "No, Mr. Bagley, I might lose it. You just keep it here."

This was, of course, no part of our business. But it heartened us.

We were fortunate in having with us both Art Krushat and Heinie Olesen. Art had been with us for years, our sailor in the desert. He took care of our business as though it were his own. "I'm not going to make a nickel on this crate of lettuce," he might grumble. But he never grumbled about all the work he had to do. His courtesy with even the most difficult customers was unfailing. He might remark, after a cantankerous man left the store, "That guy is a tomato can." Whatever that means — I took it to be sailorese. From Art it was most expressive.

Heinie Olesen had brought his wife to the desert hoping

to benefit her health. I want to tell this story in his own words because they are more vivid than mine:

"We got to Bagley's store, their home, a post office. I inquired where I could rent a small house. We rented a windmill, fixed up real nice, for $12.50 a month.

"People would look at me all so friendly and say, 'Hello.'

"The next day I went to the store to find out where I could get a job. I had heard Mr. Bagley was going to build a larger store. Who was going to build it?

"Someone said, 'See that man in white overalls? That is Mr. Berg.'

"I walked over to Mr. Berg. I told him who I was and that I wanted a job. I said, 'I am a good worker and you will be satisfied.'

"Mr. Berg looked me over and said, in his German way, 'Nicht.' He walked away. I thought, 'At least I tried.' Mr. Berg walked about fifteen feet, turned around and said, 'Come.'

"I made it in a couple of jumps. He went over to where the footing was all staked out. He said, 'Dig.'

"Boy — did I dig!"

Heinie's energy and cheer were notable. When he was no longer needed by the builder we hired him "temporarily" to help us in the store during the Christmas month and while we moved. He was with us for thirty years, and his personality contributed much to the warmth and good will people seemed to feel in the store.

Art Krushat was as conscientious about his driving as about everything else. Often our trucker would carry a passenger who had some need to make the trip. One winter day Art's passenger was a little French woman who, through years of homesteading, had managed to keep herself chic. She had delayed him in town. When finally she was ready to leave San Bernardino he pushed the rig as hard as he dared. It was raining. He made the turn onto the desert road just before it was closed by a block and a guard.

The narrow canyon in Morongo was a stream, the water gradually rising until it began to wash over the road. Art

"That it did not look like a grocery store did not immediately concern us."

"Weren't you lucky," a customer exclaimed, "to get your store right in the middle of everything!"

"Bacon Day." Waiting for truck to bring in rationed food. About 1942.

drove ahead, determined to get through with his load. The road ran along a mountainside; he edged the truck close to the mountain. Darkness came early with the storm. He jammed the wheels into the bank and stopped. They sat there all night in the drafty wet cab, uncertain whether the road would hold.

With morning light the rain stopped, the water receded to the stream bed, the wet bank held, and he made it through. Word that he was on his way had reached the store, and the men were waiting at the door of the warehouse.

They met him with relief and congratulations, discreetly hinting at romance. Art took the ribbing with a sailor's nonchalance. But he was chilled and sick. To Sarah, his wife, he confided, "I couldn't snuggle up to her like I could have to you, Mama."

He developed pneumonia and a heart condition. Dr. Luckie said that he would not be able to work again. But he did not know the spirit of the man.

After Art's ordeal Heinie and younger men took over the freighting. When the truck would be late customers might be greatly annoyed at the inconvenience — as though we were just careless. We would know that it meant trouble and extra expense. There were many flat tires and minor repairs, but we were very fortunate, for all those years and miles of travel there was only one real accident.

Rich, who had made an excellent record driving for about a year, once simply goofed, turned off the ignition in a way that caused the truck to go off the road and turn upside down. It had been an extra trip to bring in summer stock, sacks of feed, cases of pop in glass bottles, and watermelons. Our son Denny, then about ten years old, had ridden with him that day to go to his dentist in Riverside. He had been on top of the load in the back.

Rich jumped out of the cab, unhurt. He saw Denny's arm protruding from under a pile of feed sacks. Frantically he flung off the sacks, found Denny winded but whole. Had he landed under the pop cases he would have been crushed and cut.

A passing motorist promised to notify the store. While Rich and Denny waited for aid they refreshed themselves by eating broken watermelons.

We sent help to right the truck and waited anxiously. When Denny arrived I took him to one side and looked him over. He seemed intact but one ear appeared to be full of bloody pulp. "Come with me to the house, Denny," I said. "I want to wash and examine you ear."

"Oh, Mother — that is just watermelon."

I am not sure how the other men felt about that work, but for a year before he joined the Air Corps our son John drove the truck. Getting up in the dark, driving as the first lights appeared in the scattered houses, meeting no other vehicles on the lonely desert road, seeing the beauty and the freshness of the morning at dawn — he loved it.

In town the shopping was a challenge. At the produce house, owned by a Japanese he called Mr. Yamado, he was expertly helped to select new fruit and vegetables for our market. Besides doing the buying he was responsible for getting money from the bank in Beaumont, money enough to cash the pay rolls expected that week. This was routine, but hazardous.

When he drew up to the back of the warehouse the men were waiting. He would take the bills and the cash to the office and return to help with the boxes and crates. It was usually a twelve-hour day, sometimes more, but a man knew that he had done a job.

One item in our stock which did not come by truck and was most appreciated was Mrs. Janie Aaron's homemade bread. Mrs. Aaron was a little bit of a woman with shining black eyes and the brightest of smiles. She was old, and her husband was older. Tall and lank, slow of movement and speech, he had, nevertheless, an accomplishment. He knew how to build a fire for baking in a Spanish oven of stone and adobe. On their homestead, a few miles away, Janie Aaron baked in their oven bread tender and sweet with a

crisp brown crust. When you knew her and her husband
Thaddeus, the bread seemed all the more delicious.

It was hard work for both of them, and could not have
brought much proft, but they were rightly proud of it. It
was an art. When "Old Mr. Aaron" died, Janie would bake
no more. She had sons who could have helped her, but she
said no one but her husband had ever been able to make
the fire just right.

In planning this building we had tried to suggest by its
architecture the friendly atmosphere of our garage store
which had been at once our pleasure and our problem. We
did not want any prospectors from the hills to feel strange
in it. By today's standards, of course, it was an inadequate
and poor sort of a market, even though the *Desert Trail*, in a
lead article, called it a "modern supermarket."

But the benches on the long porch were enjoyed and
inside we placed several canvas chairs for people to use
while they waited or rested. The long table with a shelf underneath, which had been our first counter, we put at one
side where it could be used to assemble orders. No self-
respecting mining man would line up at a check-out
counter.

Our old customers felt a proprietary pride in the place.
Jim Hill, who hauled the lumber for our house, was a blacksmith with artistic sense. He made us a gift of two hand-
wrought iron brackets which he attached to the pillars at the
entrance to the porch. The little nursery-man found big
clay pots to fit them and kept them full of blooming
petunias. They were a spot of beauty, a token of welcome.

In a quiet corner of the main room were the shelves for
the County Branch Library, and we kept a chair there for
browsers.

This was the hardware section and less busy than other
aisles. Under adjoining shelves were open bins for nails.
Twenty years later I met an old-timer who told me that the
thing he remembered best was that I could reach into a nail
bin and pull out in my hand almost exactly one pound of

nails. What a charming accomplishment to recall to a lady passing into her declining years!

We no longer sat on dynamite boxes in the office. An adobe building for powder and a secure hiding place for caps had been constructed at a safe distance from the store. When customers brought caps to the check-out counter I got them out as fast as possible.

The bulletin board on the front of the store became a community feature. It was a large blackboard, most notices were written in chalk. We had fastened it to the garage door of the homestead store soon after we opened for business, intending to use it for ads. I think we did that only once. The board was too busy to be cluttered with mere notices of sales and prices. Once or twice Frank did write on it a list of tools and other such assets which had been borrowed or just liberated away. "Who borrowed my shovel, my tire iron, my five gallon gas can, etc., etc." A few items were returned.

Lending was a natural and almost necessary custom in pioneer life, but often highly inconvenient. Bill Smith was heard protesting to his easy-going brother Harry: "You borrowed him our saw, you borrowed away my wrench, you borrowed Al Northey my spare tire. . . ." How could the hard-working Bill build a house or drill a well or even drive to town?

A most memorable notice on the bulletin board, a year after Bill Smith had married the lovely Thelma Mead, was the announcement of the birth of their son Raymond. He was the first white child born in the community during those early years.

People wrote notices for public meetings, of weddings, deaths, and funerals. Even after the *Desert Trail* was published a notice on the board could be more timely because the newspaper was a weekly. A former editor has confided that she sometimes phoned the girl in our office and asked her to go out and look at the board to check some item which should be included in the paper.

Appeals for homes for kittens and puppies were frequently on the board. One time when it was crowded with

other notices, someone found a corner to write, "What —
no kittens!"

Typical of the neighborly spirit of the pioneer were of-
fers of rides to the city — or requests. These had always
been acceptable. But after John Hastie established his bus
route to Banning they became a problem.

John Hastie never complained, but when the dull
months of summer approached he let it be known that he
would be forced to discontinue; he did not have money
enough to carry him through the season. Other business
people who struggled through the summer understood. A
group consulted, posted a notice of a meeting on the board.
It was agreed to buy tickets for future use, to buy generously enough to carry John Hastie and his enterprise until
fall.

His service was needed. He was reliable and accom-
modating. Everyone liked him. We wanted not only the bus,
we wanted John Hastie to stay. So he did.

One of the delights of desert living is the clear night sky.
Stargazers develop a great interest in the movements of the
planets. It may suggest the cultural growth of the village
that an enthusiastic and thoughtful person printed on the
bulletin board this note: "Watch Jupiter and Venus at 4
A.M."

How many arose to view the approach of this tyrannical
father and his more or less delinquent daughter, I do not
know.

In addition to his other responsibilities Frank was now
developing our homestead land and the utilities required
for our small subdivisions. The occasional sale of a lot
helped us to pay bills.

We can laugh now about the man who had driven from
Los Angeles to buy, as previously agreed, a large lot on the
Two Mile Road. He was to pay in cash $2,000. We owed a
note for $1,997, coming due. Our prospect met us at the
store, and Frank and I, in our car led the way. The wind
was blowing. He got out of his car and we walked across the
chosen land. Frank spoke about the beautiful view, there

was no response. The wind blew harder, picking up sand. Finally the man from Los Angeles drew from his pocket a check for two thousand dollars, held it firmly while he let us read it, put it back in his pocket, and drove away.

I once showed land to a couple whose little grandchild rode with us in my car. She chattered, adult conversation was impossible. At last the grandfather firmly told her to be quiet. She was — for less than a minute. Then she said, with equal firmness, "But my mouth feels like talking."

That sale, however, was completed. Gradually, through years, we were getting out of debt.

Frank was working too hard to spend much time in the market. One day, to help me, he did the family shopping, loaded a big wire basket. As he left the store he looked at the benches on the porch, facing the sunset view. He was tired and an empty bench looked good. He would rest a few minutes, enjoy the colors of the mountains, see how it felt.

A jeep loaded with sailors from the Base on the dry lake drove up and parked. One sailor, older than most, noticed this man, twice as old as himself, grey and looking weary, sitting there with a big basket of groceries beside him. He stopped, facing Frank. With all kindness he said:

"I'll bet that old son-of-a-bitch in there makes plenty of money off guys like us."

VI. Two Men of the Mountains

Bill Keys
The Rich in Spirit

Bill Keys

It is not often that two men become friends as a result of having a collision. But that is how it happened with Frank and Bill Keys. It might be said that they met by accident.

I told the story early in this book. Driving on the single track road with the glare of the setting sun in his eyes Frank saw a small truck speeding toward him. There was a Joshua tree on his right, he pulled out to his left. Our Franklin truck was heavier; Bill Keys' truck was demolished. Yet Keys had said, "I should have seen you. I was thinking about some mining deals."

Frank had driven him to his home in the desert mountains, stayed overnight, and in the morning took him into Riverside to buy another truck. From that time they had liked and respected each other.

They had no reason or opportunity to be close friends, but Keys came to our store, and occasionally we called at his ranch when we were driving in the mountains.

I remember my first meeting with Mrs. Keys. We had been exploring caves in the wilderness and I had found a quantity of a hard black material I supposed to be a mineral. I broke off a piece and carried it with me for identification.

At Keys' Ranch she came to the gate to be introduced. "What is this, Mrs. Keys?" I asked, and I put a piece of the black stuff in her hand. She dropped it.

"Oh — that's fertilizer."

I had placed a chunk of bat guano into her bare hand.

She was a dainty woman. Living there in the mountains among boulders and piñon pines, caring for her family under primitive conditions, she kept herself and her home

neat and attractive. They had three children about the ages
of ours, and later, a baby girl.

In memory I can still visualize Bill bringing this little girl
to a community meeting at the Twentynine Palms Inn.
There he was, his gun strapped on, holding in his arms this
baby, clad in dimity and wearing a ruffled bonnet with pink
ribbons. He became impatient with the haggling over road
conditions. Finally he took the floor. "I came here to vote,"
he said. "And I want to vote." Whereupon, we did.

He used to come to the store the day before Christmas.
He would buy all the foods traditional for a feast adding
candy and other treats. And then he would add a bottle of
castor oil.

It was hard to adjust our feeling for this man as we
knew him to the tales we heard of his past. But he was a
man who belonged to the Western deserts and mountains.

William F. Keys had been born in 1879 at Palisades,
Nebraska, of Quaker parents. He had lived and worked on
their ranch until he was fifteen, and then struck out on his
own. He worked as a cowboy or in mines through the Western states. He was in the Arizona towns of Prescott and
Jerome when they were booming. Later, at Needles, he was
employed with Indians of the Walapi tribe as a cowboy and
he learned to speak their language. He hunted outlaws
along the Utah — Arizona border when serving as a deputy
sheriff at Kingman.

He turned to prospecting and joined for a time with the
legendary Scotty of Death Valley. But Scotty's chief interest
was in finding wealthy patrons, Bill's was in finding gold.
They split up and Bill dug with pick and shovel in the
Funeral Mountains.

He made some lucky strikes, and in the town of Cinco
he sent so many small shipments of gold through the post
office that the postmistress whispered around that he was a
wealthy man. He found himself socially in demand for
parties and dances. But this was not his style.

Long before Scotty was established with his legends and

his castle Keys joined him on some expeditions, and to add color let himself be known as an Indian guide.

On one such trip he was supposed to be involved in an ambush, probably staged by Scotty to make the hot and dusty trip more dramatic for his party of tenderfeet. This story is told in so many different versions that it is not worthwhile to recount it here. Keys told his daughter, years afterward, that he had spent twenty-nine days in a Barstow jail, then was cleared by a group of witnesses who swore that he had been in camp at the time of the ambush.

He came near to this area in 1910 when he hired on as a cowboy at Surprise Spring. A year later he moved to the mountains which are now known as the territory of the Joshua Tree National Monument. There he worked the Tully Mine and milled his ore in Twentynine Palms. He made $100 a ton, but the pocket soon ran out. He moved to the Desert Queen Mine, which had been worked and then lost by Jim and Bill McHaney. He did assessment work for the owner and acted as watchman.

This is one of the most beautiful parts of the desert mountains; rugged with giant boulders and rich with Joshua trees, piñon pine and juniper. There he filed on eighty acres as a homestead which included a mill site for processing ore, and he stocked it with cattle. He was thirty-seven years old then, and he had been always a wanderer and an adventuring man.

Now on a trip to Los Angeles he met Frances Lawton. They were married and he brought her to the Desert Queen Ranch. They made it a home.

Bill continued his interest in prospecting and cattle; now he also developed his ranch. Through the years he enlarged his house and added other buildings. He constructed dams to form reservoirs which held the snows of winter and provided water for his cattle through the long hot summers. He made roads. One road, of which he was proud, is about ten miles long; it leads from his ranch to a spectacular view of the Coachella Valley, the Salton Sea, and to the mountains of Mexico a hundred miles away. This site is now called "Key's View."

As his family grew he planted an orchard and a vegetable garden and sold the surplus to a store in Yucca Valley. When the children were of school age he set aside one cabin for a schoolroom and hired a teacher.

At about this time Frank had an experience which enabled him to understand some of Keys' problems and incidents which occurred later. I have spoken of Fred, a miner, a graduate of Heidelberg University in Germany, who had fallen on hard days and was trying to recoup his fortunes by prospecting. He believed he had a valuable claim, was working it alone, and he feared he was about to be hi-jacked. Frank suspected that Fred had been in trouble with the law, he was so careful of transgressing. Fred asked Frank to go with him to the sheriff of San Bernardino County and ask for protection.

They drove the one hundred miles to the sheriff's office and Fred told of the threats he had received. The sheriff listened, asked a few questions; then he said, "You have a gun, haven't you?"

"Yes," Fred admitted.

"Do you know how to use it?"

"Yes."

"Well, it would not be possible in this huge county to guard every digging, every prospector who feels that he is in danger. It is up to you to take care of yourself."

A few weeks later we drove one Sunday afternoon through the beautiful cool country around Keys' ranch. On a fence we saw this sign:

"Homer Urton. KEEP OUT.
You will be shot on sight."

We thought it was funny, an absurd reminder of the old West. We laughed.

Later we heard — perhaps from Bill Keys himself — that Urton worked for a large cattle ranch in Yucca Valley. In the summer he let his cattle range in the mountains

Bill Keys. "He was a man who belonged to the western deserts and mountains. He had no time to waste in bitterness."

National Park Service photos

Below: Key's Ranch. "The land remained, the beautiful rugged land his home."

where there was forage. They got into Keys' fenced land; Urton cut the wires to let them through and allowed Keys' animals, including his milch cow, to go with them.

Probably Urton knew of the sign, and went back prepared for trouble. Keys shot him in the gun arm. Brought to trial he was acquitted on grounds of self defense.

On one of his visits to our store Bill Keys told Frank that he had personally confronted the county Board of Supervisors and had told them:

"I am giving you notice that I will not pay this tax bill or any other from the county. I receive no service. The roads I use I built myself. I have no protection. Worst of all, no school is provided for my children."

The supervisors respected the logic of Bill's defiance. His cabin was declared an "emergency school" and a teacher was sent. His two youngest children and four from neighboring homesteads made up the required enrollment of six, and sometimes the children of miners' families attended.

The teacher sent them was a Mrs. Howard Dudley who had been a missionary in Burma for thirty years. Her husband lived with her on the ranch. They were gracious and kind. They liked the Keys' family and they taught not only the subjects of the curriculum but their own wide vision of the world.

This effort to assure the education of their children speaks for the character of Bill and Frances. He had developed into the type of pioneer who build self reliance and strength into his family and community.

When the Joshua Tree National Monument was formed in 1936, its territory surrounded Keys' land. Bright young men in uniform called to tell him what he could do and could not do with his ranch and roads. Naturally Bill resented them, but he adapted. His life had never been easy. He was reasonable with new neighbors and often helpful. Their children were welcome in the school he had built. When a man named Worth Bagley bought a large tract of land adjoining the Keys' ranch, Frances and Bill tried to be friendly.

Worth Bagley came to our store in Twentyine Palms and called on Frank. They discussed their name and the possibility that they were related. They found no evidence of family connection, and I think they were both glad.

To avoid confusion I shall now, in this narrative, call Worth Bagley merely Worth.

He told Frank that he was a retired Los Angeles policeman of some rank, and that he had moved to the desert for his health. He seemed a harsh and haughty man. However, he casually admitted that he was an expert shot and a member of a famous marksman's club. Several of the men who frequented our village center were good shots, and they used to amuse themselves, while waiting for mail, by shooting at targets and tin cans. Worth drew his own pistol from a holster and started a can rolling over the uneven ground of a vacant lot. He kept it in motion, although it bumped and jumped, he never missed a shot.

Both Worth and Bill Keys talked to Frank about a dispute they had over a road. The road had been built by the McHaney brothers when they operated the Desert Queen Mine fifty years before. Bill Keys used it almost daily when he went to a well from which, with a gasoline engine, he pumped water for his cattle. The road did cross Worth's land. Worth became more and more hostile. Bill even consulted the officials of the Monument about his right. They assured him, as Frank had done, that under the California Law of Eminent Domain a road which had been used by the public for five years, unless it has been posted as private property cannot be closed.

Worth complained bitterly to Frank across the counter one day. Frank said:

"Bill Keys is in his right. Under the law of Eminent Domain he can continue his use of that road. There is no way you can stop him."

Worth exploded. "The hell I can't! I can kill him!"

One day in May of 1943 Bill Keys came to the office of

our store and asked for Frank. The girl in the office, Carmen, had been with us only a short time and did not know him. She told him courteously that Mr. Bagley had not yet come in.

"I want to see him," insisted Bill Keys. "I have just killed a man and I want him to go my bond."

Carmen supposed he was joking, so she laughed politely.

Keys left and went to the office of Judge Poste, our justice of the peace. He repeated his statement to Dave Poste and again asked that Frank be called.

Dave Poste phoned Frank, "Bill Keys is here and wants to see you."

When Frank entered the office, which was also the phone office, Anna had taken over the switchboard and was putting through a call to Jack Cones, the constable. Dave and Bill were sitting quietly.

Keys said to Frank, "I have shot Worth. I want you to go my bond."

"Did you kill him?"

"I think so," said Bill. "I watched him for about twenty minutes and he did not move."

Neither man knew that in such a case, suspicion of murder, a "bond" cannot be accepted.

Dave Poste notified Sheriff Shay of San Bernardino County and gave Keys into the custody of Constable Cones. Shay met them in the mountains, at the site of the fight. They found Worth lying face down in the sand, his gun in his hand. It was cocked and one bullet was missing. There were no foot prints but his own near the body.

Bill told them this. He had gone that morning to the well to pump water for his cattle. He was expecting a herd of cattle from their winter range, and must be prepared. He had trouble with the pump engine, the magneto was weak; he put it in his car and started for his house, about two miles distant, to get another. Worth had seen him at the well, and he had brought from his house a hammer, material for a sign, and his gun.

When Keys approached the line between the two properties he saw a Joshua tree log across the road, with a large
card nailed to it. He got out of his car and walked up to the
sign to read it. It said:

> "Keys. This is my last warning.
> Keep off my property."

Worth was across the rise in the road, tugging at
another log. He did not see Keys, who got back to his car
and reached in for his Remington. As he turned, Worth
came over the log, his six-shooter at the ready in his hand.
He saw Keys and came on, stooping. He shot. The bullet
missed Keys' head, left its mark by the door of his car.

Bill Keys said, "I shot immediately at the gun, missed it,
but grazed his arm."

Worth jumped, whirled on his heel, and came on with
his gun over his head.

Bill shot three times, hitting Worth in the side. "He fell
to the ground."

Bill Keys watched but did not go near the body. Then
he drove by a roundabout road to his house and got a new
magneto.

There was no one at the house. Frances and the children were living in town where the older children were
going to school. So Bill got himself a bite of lunch, found a
new magneto, and returned — again round-about, started
the pump and filled the water tank. When the tanks were
full, ready for his cattle, he drove to Twentynine Palms to
turn himself over to the authorities. He knew he might be
gone a long time.

The jurors at his subsequent trial were prejudiced by the
fact that he had gone about filling his tanks. To Bill it was
the merciful and necessary thing to do. There had been a
fight and he had killed the man who wanted to kill him.
The cattle would be thirsty.

This fight had taken place at the line between Riverside
and San Bernardino counties — a line little noted on maps.

It required a survey to determine that Bill should be tried in Riverside County.

The trial was long, lacking in definite proofs. Bill was tried for murder; he claimed self-defense. The jury brought in a compromise verdict, manslaughter. The sentence was "from five years to life."

It is painful even to imagine what prison meant to Bill Keys. Cold grey walls shutting a man who had lived in wild places and among the boulders and canyons of Queen Valley. The stink of prison to one who had breathed sunny air and the fragrance of pines and junipers. The intolerable loneliness of a crowd to a father who had loved his home and children.

He was offered parole and he refused it. He felt that to accept the restrictions of parole would be to admit guilt. He protested his innocence and remained in prison.

Frances Keys' loyalty sustained him. She was a shy woman, yet she came to our store and stood on the porch, asking for signatures to a petition praying the governor for a full pardon. When it failed, she turned to Erle Stanley Gardner, the famous attorney and detective story writer who loved the desert, often camped in its mountains and knew the Keys family. He understood the circumstances of Bill's conviction and he admired Mrs. Keys' quiet charm and courage. He was deeply concerned about men unjustly imprisoned and was devoting himself to "The Court of Last Resort." He studied such cases and published the stories in *Argosy* magazine.

Gardner found men who were experts in detection and in analyzing evidence. They studied the five bound volumes of Keys' trial proceedings. They also discovered an affidavit made by Worth's former wife telling of his mental aberration, his impulse to kill. These had never been introduced at the trial. Erle Stanley Gardner came to believe that Keys had indeed shot in self-defense. He then got a hearing with the California Adult Authority, the board which determines paroles. They could not pardon, but they agreed that an error had been made. Gardner then persuaded Keys to accept their parole offer. A pardon from the governor might come later.

Bill Keys accepted the parole and went home to the Desert Queen Ranch among the Joshua trees. He had been four and a half years in prison. His cattle had been sold to pay the lawyers. But the land remained, the beautiful rugged land, his home. And Frances was there.

He was seventy years old, but still wiry and strong. He cleared the dams, repaired the roads. He had no time to waste in bitterness.

There was also gold to find. He went prospecting, and now that the children were grown, Frances could go with him.

However, he wanted not only this liberty but a full pardon. He wanted to remove the stigma of his prison sentence from his family and he was determined to be a citizen again, to vote and take part in public affairs.

It was July of 1956, a hot day but pleasant there in the desert mountains. Frances and he were sitting together under their piñon pine trees. A messenger brought Bill Keys a sealed document. He looked at the seal and knew it was from the governor. He handed it to Frances.

"Here, Mother," he said.

She opened and read to him the full and unconditional pardon of the Governor of the State of California.

The Rich in Spirit

We had been keeping store in the desert for enough years so that we were used to people who live in the wide spaces. Yet when I first saw Sally I stared at her, not quite believing.

My husband and I were working in our back room office when John Olson and Sally came into the empty store. We heard her voice, pitched high and thin, like that of a very little girl.

"Just look, John!" she was saying. "Here's a library — and shoes and water bags — and silk stockings — and candy! Why haven't we been here before?"

I went out to wait on them. Sally's back was turned and I had time to stare. She had the body of an old woman, thick and coarse. She wore what were called pajamas, a two-legged flowing garment made of pink flowered muslin. Over the gay pajamas was a man's coat, patched at the elbows, and on her feet, men's shoes. Her hat was a farmer's straw; she had trimmed it with flowers and cock's feathers. She was so curious and so delighted with the jumbled variety of our country store that she did not see me. I was quite aware that the place looked like an Irish stew, that in its own way it was quite as odd as she. To have someone so appreciative was very pleasant.

She turned around. "I'm Sally," she said. "What's your name?" She smiled like a friendly child. Her prominent blue eyes, round and wondering, were incongruous in a face weathered by desert winds and lined with the inclemencies of fifty years.

John Olson spoke. "Is this your store, missus? Where is the mister? Ve come to trade and ve vant some shells for my gun and some powder for the mine. Aye, but I do not see dynamite."

"The shells are over here by the ladies' stockings," I said. "The dynamite is in the office. It's safer there, and we can sit on the boxes.

"Aye," said John gravely. "Sometimes ve are crowded at my place too. Ve hide it from the goats, under the bed."

Frank came out and was introduced. John said, "My name is Olson. This lady, Sally Hart, she keeps my house. First ve pay for the powder. Then ve know how much ve can buy."

John was as grave as Sally was exuberant. His speech was difficult to understand, for although he had been many years from the old country he had not practiced unnecessarily. He was about sixty years old, but his face was less wrinkled than Sally's. His blue eyes under grizzled brows were quiet, his mouth firm and kind. His frame had settled to stockiness, but he was not stooped. He had the poise of a man whose strength and wealth are sufficient for his needs.

"We used to go to Banning," Sally was prattling happily, "but they don't have things for the mine. John mines pretty rocks; they use them in churches and libraries. The stores are bigger in Banning, but they don't keep so much all together. Just look, John, there's a nice shiny meat case, and there's your tobacco on the shelves right behind it. And see all the different kinds of beans!

"I used to go to a store like this when I was a little girl — " She stopped her chatter and a shadow crossed her face. "Was that a long time ago? I remember I had a baby doll once — she had a pink dress — it was the only baby I ever had."

John and Frank had been assembling staple foods on the counter. Coffee, beans, rice and flour. "Canned milk?" Frank suggested.

"No, ve haf the goats. A piece of bacon maybe. Would you please count it up and see how much? Sally, she vould like some candy."

Sally chose her candy with the eager discrimination of a

five year old. "John always buys me candy," she confided in her treble voice. "Sometimes he forgets tobacco." When Frank packed their box he added candy bars and I slipped in a store cake. It probably tasted like sawdust, but it gleamed richly through its cello wrappings and Sally had been eyeing it with wistful greediness.

John saw the cake. "Thank you, missus," he said, accepting gravely. "Some day you come to see us. Soon ve have some string beans in our garden. Aye, Sally, she always glad to have company."

One hot Sunday in June we drove to see Sally and John. To go to Pipes Canyon we traveled west on the road toward Banning nearly as far as the village called Yucca, and then we turned north into the highlands. At once the air was cooler; there were juniper and scrub oak among the Joshua trees. We followed a creek bed, and then, at about five thousand feet, a stream. The road forded it through a thicket of desert willow. Once we left the car to admire the little orchid-like blossoms of the willow, and to look for the prints of deer hoofs in the mud.

The trail was rocky and steep, but the piñon pines, the willows, the junipers loaded with grey-green berries, made a different land. We could smell the water, and hear it as we drove along; the fragrance of the pines was enchanting.

Then we came to a house, a sprawling rock house, set into the rocky slope of the mountainside above the road. Sally had heard the noise of the climbing car and was watching from the door.

"You're the store people, aren't you? My, isn't this nice!"

Goats and kids, excited and curious, appeared from rocks and bushes. There was no use trying to count them; kids are in so many places at once. We lost the fragrance of the pines. Chickens and ducks came clucking and quacking. Sally shooed at them with her apron made from the back of a man's blue work shirt.

"Go way," she said, and in the same breath, "aren't they cute! They love to see people. I'll give you a kid to take home with you. I always hate to eat them. Oh, here's John now."

He appeared from the direction of the creek below. "Gude day, Mr. Bagley," he said. "Gude day, Missus. We are happy to have you come. Vould you see my garden? Aye, it is gude you come today. I give you my first radishes."

Followed by goats and chickens we crossed the road and went down a short trail. Beside the bed of the stream there was an enclosure fenced with brush and watered by an ingenious wheel which lifted water from the creek and poured it into ditches. The garden was less than a quarter acre but in our country it seemed a wonder.

John carefully closed the gate to keep out the goats and chickens. "It's too bad," shrilled Sally. "They are always so disappointed."

Leaf lettuce, radishes, young turnips. John and Sally pulled them as they talked. "For you to take home," Sally told us happily.

I protested. "But you have worked so hard to grow them. We have vegetables in our store, you know."

"Not like these," said John gently. And then, "Excuse me, Missus.

"You see my vater vheel? Such a vheel I helped my father make in the old country. For me it sings."

"Nearly every spring the water smashes it," babbled Sally. "We used to have our cabin here. The yellow monkey flowers and the paint brush bloomed so pretty right beside it. But after the big snow it washed away. John never cussed a bit! Just set up a tent for me and laid out our new house the next day. I never saw a man work like he does!"

"Did you do all this and build your house alone?" asked Frank.

"No, Sally she help me with the fence. Ve built it as soon as the vater had gone down, so I could plant my garden. Then I made a new vater vheel. When it does not squeak the land seems strange. Aye, it is like voman's talk — a com-

fortable sound." He glanced toward Sally and his grave face
crinkled. "A man does not need to listen to the vords."

"Then I just mine a while to get out the onyx. My mine
it is farder up the road. In vinter the snow comes ve cannot
get the rock out, and ve must have a little money. In the
summer I vork the mine. But nights I build on the house."

"I want to show you our house," urged Sally.

John continued modestly. "Carl and Pete, they are my
partners in the mine. They help me too. But after supper
they vant to smoke and sleep. I smoke a little."

"John worked at night," said Sally.

"Aye, it is gude to vork in the moonlight. It is right that
a man make shelter for himself."

For a man working in the moonlight the house was a
considerable achievement. It was built of rocks against the
side of a hill so that the natural boulders formed part of the
structure. There was a living room, a bedroom and a
kitchen, and off the kitchen a cave. Sally led us to the cave.
This was her storage room, her special pride. She must
show us everything — the goat's milk cooling in the crocks,
the cheese stored along the shelves, the dried fruits, the
basket of eggs. The good smells of cheese, of homemade
bread, and the spicy fragrance of dried apricots all mingled
with the odor of the earth from which they came.

When we left we had to take gifts of leaf lettuce,
radishes, goat's milk and cookies. We managed not to accept
a kid. It was scrambling over the hood of our car and Sally
insisted we should take it to our boys. Only the argument
that it might be run over in the village persuaded her not to
put it in our car.

I never learned much of the history of John and Sally.
She had once run a tavern in the mountains of San Bernardino County and she had been considered competent and
successful. I do not know what happened to change her to
the childless child we knew. Thanks to John, she was a
happy child.

John had been tempered by some old grief of which he
would not talk. I think it was the shadow of old sorrow

which caused him to open his door to receive the tragic agent of his death.

They came to trade about once a month. When we built our new store Sally took a personal pride in it. Frank was usually busy in his office, a few steps from the main part of the building with a door between. But when Sally came to market he would hear her little girl treble —

"Where's Frank? We haven't seen him for so long! I want to thank him for that pretty cake he put in our box. I never knew it was there until we got home."

Frank usually came down to wait on them himself. Trips to the store are social events to people who live out in the desert mountains. The strangers in the place would be staring delightedly; tourists are always hoping to see characters.

Sally had become even more simple in mind, but she was pathetically very much a woman. She added flounces to the legs of her pink pajamas and streamers to the straw hat.

Sometime every summer we would drive to Pipes Canyon and call on John and Sally. "Look," she would say, "do sign my guest book. Write something pretty."

A visitor of rare insight had sent her a large guest book. If we made a ceremony of writing our names and pleasant messages it was possible to leave without partaking of refreshments. Sally's housekeeping had not improved. After we had seen her puppy asleep on what appeared to be a large soft cushion and discovered that it was a pan of rising dough covered with a towel we were glad to leave the stone house without drinking goat's milk and eating home baking. But not even a stranger could come and go without some gift of vegetables or fruit or a piece of choice onyx from the mine.

When war came restrictions made it impossible for John to work his mine, because he could not get priorities for steel and powder. They lived more meagerly. But his hardships seemed to him to be of small concern. Across our grocery counter, where we had so often listened to the complaints of the well-to-do, John said, "Lots of young fellers in the var — in the prison camps — young fellers are the ones who need to eat. Aye, they vould tink ve eat like kings, Sally and me. Aye, I knew a young feller once . . ." He said no more. When he saw Frank add tobacco to his box of groceries he could only nod his thanks.

Across a grocer's counter a man may speak from his heart, but one does not ask questions across a counter.

Sally had been standing beside John, her round eyes wide and shining. She waited until he had gone out with his box, and then she followed Frank as he went to his office.

"Oh, Mr. Bagley," she confided, and her shrill voice could be heard to the end of the store. "The most wonderful thing has happened! I'm going to have a baby!"

Fortunately for Frank's composure, John returned and gently led her away.

Within a few days a letter came from Sally. It was neatly written in a hand that had once been skilled.

"Dear Mr. Bagley,

John doesn't know that I told you what I did about having a baby. But he says it isn't so. He says it is all in my head.

Please don't tell him what I said to you. If he knew he wouldn't let me come to your store anymore. And I do like to come to your store better than any place.

Yours respectfully,
Sally"

She deteriorated rapidly after that. She had a stroke and could walk and talk only with great difficulty. John was advised to take her to the county hospital, but he refused. "You say they could not make her young again. Could they make her happy? No. Ve get along."

He would guide her around the store. Once he had to ask for the "ladies room." He never betrayed embarassment or impatience or even pity. But Sally's eyes were bewildered. The next stroke was fatal. John closed the eyes with silver coins.

He was left alone in the stone house in Pipes Canyon. During the war few people passed that way. It was winter and the water wheel was silent. Like Sally's prattle, it had been a comfortable sound.

By chance a young man came to his door. He was a soldier, returned from the slaughter of combat and due for a medical discharge. But to his tortured mind even a few more days in camp had become intolerable. He was running away, and he seemed to have found the perfect hiding place. John gladly took him in and asked no questions. He wore part of a uniform and John had much to share.

The soldier remained about two weeks.

One day a neighbor came, saw no smoke from the chimney and opened the door. John had been shot. He had been lying on his bed, without food, for three days. Mercifully he had reached a little water.

The soldier, he said, had shot him with his own gun. He had taken the food from the storage cave and left him, wounded.

John was carried to the county hospital. He lived a few days longer in pain and weakness. The soldier was found living in a mine shaft in the canyon, eating the food from John's house. He had the gun.

The sheriff came to get a statement from John.

John knew that he was dying — the other man might live. "It vas an accident," he swore. "He was sitting there across from me. I gave him the gun, he vas cleaning it. Aye, it yust vent off. It vas an accident. The poor young feller!"

And that was the last thing John Olson had to give.

VII. The Base on the Dry Lake

The War Years

They shone like silver in the deep blue air, silent, free as birds. In thermals they circled and climbed; they soared, casting swift shadows across bare desert mountains and parched white sands.

Beautiful — oh beautiful — if only they flew for peace.

The young men who flew the gliders believed they flew for peace. To renew it for the far-off countries of Europe, convulsed in the horrors of war and bound by Hitler's occupation. These glider pilots loved adventure, the poetry of flight. They also loved freedom so well that they relinquished their own, hoping to share it with other lands.

They learned to control and direct this silent flight, realizing that they must one day use it for combat, to glide through dark nights to conquer sleeping villages — perhaps in Normandy — to surprise and kill other men who also had strength and courage.

All this they knew and put from their thoughts. Their skill was duty.

They were so young, so strictly disciplined. Our town of Twentynine Palms had little to offer by way of diversion. Saturday they would come to the store, buy iced watermelons, cut them in pieces, and sit on the curb to eat them, careful not to get one drop of juice on neat khaki uniforms. I used to imagine the catastrophe if an officer came by and they rose to salute. But if any officer drove up, he kindly looked the other way and did not stop.

Condor Field was a major glider base. It had been installed in November of 1941, a few days before Pearl Harbor. In 1942 it was commanded by Captain L. C. Hess. Colonel Benioff, our friend of homestead days, told me that the Air Force had spent a year investigating the western part of the

United States before selecting the site. During that time there were reported only five days when gliders could not have flown.

There were other outfits in training. Patton's army was being toughened for the invasion of Africa on the sands and mountains of the Mojave. From Iron Mountain they moved across the harsh terrain of the Coxcombs as far as Eagle Mountain. It was whispered that men had died in the oven of the tanks.

Late one evening two soldiers came to the door of our house. One said, "Would you open your store and send a man to sell us some lunch meats? Our company had only jelly sandwiches today."

"I can do it," I said.

I unlocked the store and went behind the meat counter. The night was cold; both men wore long drab coats but they smelled of the heat and sweat of the day. I could see no insignia.

I got out bologna and ham and put them on the slicer which had to be turned by hand. The younger and taller man came around the counter. "If I may, — I will turn that for you." The other man stood across the meat case. He ordered what to cut.

When the meat had been cut and wrapped it was the man who had turned the slicer who signed the check, "Captain — ."

He was a considerate man, and kind. He must have driven more than one hundred miles that cold night, in his jeep, to find something better than jelly for his men. Soon he would be leading them, in another desert, into a hell of tank warfare, crashing steel and flame.

General Patton's headquarters had been near Iron Mountain, about fifty miles east of Twentynine Palms. After his army had left, we visited the site. A relief map had been made in the sand reinforced with concrete. On it were shown the hills and roads of the region. These could be studied from an elevated walk. It had been used to train observers in reading natural features of landscape.

The streets of the camp had been neatly lined with pieces of white quartz. Busy occupation for homesick boys.

All debris and lumber had been removed. There remained only the altars of two chapels, altars built and arched with the gleaming white quartz. Stark against the desert sand and mountains, they remain as a memorial for men who had prayed there, prayed that they might return some day to a land of trees and flowers and gentle ways — or to die bravely.

After the invasion of Normandy, D Day, the glider base was closed. It had been the largest in the United States, but its purpose had been accomplished. In March of 1943 the Twentynine Palms Air Academy was designated a Primary Power School; training planes replaced the gliders.

One day I was waiting on two young sergeants at the counter. They had just received orders to remain for three more weeks at the desert base, and they were discussing their fate in tones of outrage. I looked up from the sales slip I was writing. "Be careful," I said. "If you stay three months you will not want to leave at all."

They stared at me, incredulous. One asked, "How long have you been here?"

"Seventeen years."

He turned to his fellow sergeant. "Gosh! Here we was griping about three weeks, — and she has been here — seventeen years."

No printed words can convey the inflections of horror and pity in his voice. It so happened that they did remain three more months, and they did not want to go.

For a time the Navy took over the base. Sailors found it hard to adjust to duty on a dry lake.

The cadets had addressed us "Sir" and "Ma'am." One of the first sailors, calling me, said, "Hey, chicken." I tried to freeze him.

"Were you speaking to me? I was not sure because I am not accustomed to being spoken to that way."

Later, with no intended disrespect, I was called, "Hey,

Mom." I decided that I preferred the former endearment.
They were all friendly and warmhearted.

To cadet fliers the desert must have appeared very large
and bare. Away from the village of Twentynine Palms there
were great spaces with only scattered cabins.

Adelaide Arnold, author and poet, lived in one of these.
She was old and gentle. Her face was deeply lined with the
sorrows and emotions of many years. She would never tell
how many. She wrote industriously for her income was
meager. The things she cherished were all in that cabin in
the sands.

One day, a cadet, feeling free and joyous, swooped
down to have a look. He buzzed, and the shock of his flight
knocked Adelaide's old china from the shelves and shattered cups upon the floor. Adelaide was a patriot, but this
was too much.

She got into her car and drove directly to the Base. She
demanded, yes demanded, to see the commander. He
would find the flier and discipline him — he promised. She
went home and waited, sitting with the shattered china
around her on the floor.

There came a knock. She pulled herself to her full five
feet and opened the door. The boy who stood there was
straight and tall, but so young, and ashamed. She let him
come in and he asked if he could at least pick up the pieces.
Still angry she gave him a dust pan and a basket. But there
was so much of it, Adelaide got down and helped.

When the floor was cleared she invited him to stay for
tea. She used the daintiest things she had left and brewed
her finest tea.

What were old cups compared to this young life?

They were friends, they exchanged addresses, and when
he was in Europe, flying in combat, they wrote to each
other.

We were proud, as a community, of the boys from our
town. Because there were so many who enlisted I can write
only of those who were closest to our family.

The older sons went first. Derald Martin and Bill

Derald Martin, John Bagley and Ray Flickinger met in Hawaii.

Alan Bagley, B29 Pilot.

Denny Bagley, Naval Aviation.

Krushat flew transport planes to the South Pacific. Chandler Flickinger fought in Europe, was wounded in the Battle of the Vosges Mountains in Alsace-Lorraine. After he recovered from his wound he was transferred to the Army Intelligence Corps. For this service he was awarded the Legion of Merit. He says, "It was for a fairly good job by the Counter Intelligence, rather than by me, but you can't decorate everybody."

Harold Hockett, the only son of early homesteaders, Ivy and Bill Hockett, who were so helpful to us in the early days of our venture in desert living, enlisted in the air corps and served as a pilot.

Troy Martin came to me. I had known him since he was five. There was a new manliness about him; tall, with reddish hair and a matching sprinkle of freckles across his nose.

"Mrs. Bagley," he said, "I am applying for the air corps. Will you write a letter of recommendation for me?"

"Oh, Troy, your mother already has one son who is a flyer. Isn't that enough?"

"Mrs. Bagley, it is something I have wanted all my life."

I wrote the letter. If I did not, someone else would.

Alan and he were friends. Alan left Cal Tech for the air corps.

Stanley Krushat became a bombardier. The youngest Krushat son, Lester, enlisted in the Navy as soon as he was old enough. His father, Art, who had been our store manager for years, had kept his reserve status. He returned to service as Chief Gunner's Mate. Sarah moved to San Diego to be near him. She worked in a parachute shop.

Our store put up a service flag with two stars, for Art and John. John, our eldest son, who had been working with Frank, driving the truck for the market, and doing the buying, had enlisted with Stan.

Ruefully he said, "I can't feel any enthusiasm for killing Japanese. The only one I know is Yamado, the wholesale produce man, and he is one of the nicest guys I ever met."

Ray Flickinger, Jr. went into training for naval aviation,

the V 5. His father, Ray, Sr., joined the Navy. He said, "I was too young for the first world war, and I am almost too old for this. My boys are in it. I want to have a part."

Boot camp was rough for him. Boys younger than his own, enjoying his humor and his grit, cheered him on. "Hey, Pop — you made it."

He was assigned to post office work in Hawaii.

Denny, as soon as he finished high school, tried to enlist in the Marines. He was rejected because his arches were too high. Strange, I thought, for a boy who had gone barefoot, worn tennis shoes, and hiked so much. He joined the V 5 training for naval aviation.

Our home had three stars on its service flag.

John, Alan, and Troy were together at Santa Ana for the second stage of their training. On the first weekend that they were privileged to have visitors they asked us to come to the camp. Troy's parents, Tom and Maude Martin joined us there. We sat together in a circle on the lawn of the hostess house. John said, "Dad, will you and mother please sit together." Our sons presented us with a chest of silver. It was our twenty-fifth wedding anniversary.

John and Alan graduated together. They came home with silver wings.

Troy Martin had completed his training. He was in camp at Santa Maria when his group was ordered to March Field, near Riverside, to take altitude tests. There was just time for him to hitchhike to Twentynine Palms for a farewell visit. Returning to the transport plane he was late by a few minutes. He caught a ride with a trucker who was driving at night and barely made the field in Santa Maria in time for roll call. He ran to line up.

The officers stared at him. Apprehenisve about his appearance, he pulled himself straighter; they continued to stare. They thought they were seeing a ghost. The transport plane with his comrades had crashed in the mountains near Santa Barbara, with no survivors.

His parents, Maude and Tom Martin, felt that a special providence had spared their son. They were deeply grateful. He went overseas. Based in Hollandia, West Irian, he flew over New Guinea from April to June. Then came the telegram. Lt. Martin, returning from a combat mission with a damaged plane, had crashed in the jungle. There was an agony of uncertainty, of waiting. Waking in the night, imagining him wounded or a prisoner, trapped. What would it be like? But still a gleam of hope. A final message: his body had been recovered.

Stanley Krushat, on a bombing mission over the Ploesti oil fields in Rumania, was shot down and captured. The message was delivered to his parents in San Diego. Sarah told me afterwards, "Art was due at his station. He went to work. And I — I cleaned cupboards all night."

John had flown a two engine B-25 to Hawaii. His unit had been forced to wait two weeks for the necessary tail wind. If the wind should fail their fuel would not get them to Hawaii. From there they flew to the Philippines. His missions were from Palawan over Borneo, bombing anti-aircraft defenses in the jungles. He wrote, "Sometimes we find bits of treetops, even long grass, in the propeller when we return."

Alan had qualified as pilot of the four-engine B-29. He told us, "It is like sitting on the front porch of a seven-room house and taking it up." For a time, still in this country, he was stationed at a field where he could use a car, and John's was available. But before he could take the car into the field, Frank and I had to go before a notary and sign an affidavit, giving our consent, because he was not yet twenty-one years old.

We were anxious and sad. We had a sensitive awareness, not only for our friends, for all the servicemen — no matter how brash they seemed — including the strangers who passed through our doors. Who could know what burden of grief a stranger might be carrying?

I was in the store one day, doing work John or Art would have done. I became conscious of a blue uniform. I looked up to see Lester Krushat smiling down at me. Lester,

Lieutenant Troy Martin
June 25, 1923 — June 11, 1944
"They shall grow not old
As we who are left grow old."

Below: Stanley Krushat with Sarah and Art after his return. "Remember, it was their first chance to get back at us."

so young, happy and proud, with a new red insignia of rank on his sleeve.

I said, "Why, Lester — you dear child!"

I think he did not notice, or if he did he forgave me, for he stayed in our home and spent happy days listening to records on the old victrola Alan had wired. He was to go across the ocean soon to fly in a T.B.F. torpedo bomber which had no escape hatch for the gunner's compartment.

The next time I see Lt. Colonel Krushat, now of the Army Air Force, I shall ask him if he noticed.

Stanley Krushat had been imprisoned in Bucharest from May to October of 1944. When he came home, Stan, who had always been so kind, so full of fun, looked like a man who had been beaten. Indeed, he had been beaten with his hands tied behind him, by the gendarmes who came to capture him. They had beaten the bomber crew with rifle butts all the way to prison.

His mother, Sarah, remembers, "We were talking in the kitchen, the first evening he was at home. I burst out, 'Don't tell me any more. I can't bear it." Stan looked at me quizzically, and then he said:

" 'You have to remember, Mother, — we had been bombing them for two weeks. This was their first chance to get back at us.' "

He was never as jolly and carefree again, but he was mature and wise.

The American Legion Post in Twentynine Palms, had been named the Desert Outpost. After the war the name was changed to Troy L. Martin Post. Maude organized the Gold Star Mothers in the town.

The Boys from Our Town

These had been the little fellows starting school.
The scrubbed-for-Sunday boys who sang so well —
"Onward Christian Soldiers."
The brown swimmers, heels up in the pool,
the Boys Scouts learning to bivouac,
playing sand-lot baseball,
dashing around
in incredible jalopies crowded with their kind.

They had been graduating from high school or college,
planning careers, working at their first jobs.
Some of them had sweethearts, wives.

But they were not too young to accept
the heavy duty of the war.
They loved fair play and freedom.
Courage and honor had become as essential to them
as sunshine and wide spaces.

Now they endured the monotonous voyage,
the strain and tension of flight,
the fatigue of the forced march,
the misery of fox holes and jungles,
the madness of battle.
Wounds, imprisonment and death
had been the lot of some.
The record of their honors is long.

They fought well.
They helped bring victory and peace.
All but a few returned, returned to live
with qualities of courage and honor
as they had fought.
And we knew that our sons were men,
our boys and the neighbor boys
were men.

The Glider Pilot

Vinton Harz came to Condor Field, the glider base at the dry lake near Twentynine Palms, in June of '42. He was athletic, alert, as a pilot must be. He had a shock of hair the color of sun burned galleta grass. His blue eyes seemed always to be opened especially wide, as though he found life surprising and did not want to miss anything. He enjoyed flying and was very good at it.

In September he met Lois Marlow and was invited to her home. Lois had grown up on her father's homestead near the dry lake. The previous year she had attended college in San Bernardino, but in the summer she worked in an office on the base. Lois decided not to return to college that fall.

She was eighteen and lovely, with a special quality of serenity and strength — excellent traits for a woman who loves an airman. They were married in January. Lois confides, "I had never supposed I could possibly marry after so short an engagement — but it has lasted."

They had one weekend of honeymoon and then Vinton returned to duty at Victorville. He had been assigned to training other pilots, but scarlet fever of the old-fashioned virulent type with complications forced him into the hospital. He was there seventy-two days. Lois and he visited through a window. It seemed that he might never fly again.

When he recovered and passed as fit for duty he was sent to other training fields in the United States. Lois went along, cheerfully accepting the inconveniences of camp quarters; aware, as war brides are, that time for companionship is precious. When Vinton shipped from New York Port of Embarkation in April of '44 she returned to the desert, a "lady in waiting," waiting for a child to be born sometime in June.

For Vinton there was further training in England and the tense waiting for the day of invasion, the flight for which he had been skilled and hardened. D Day, June 6, 1944, he was towed across the channel for attack.

The glider he piloted for combat was not the silver-shining craft of the training field. It was a British-built Horsa. It had a wing span of 101 feet and was designed to carry as much as a ton. His was loaded with a jeep, a trailer, and five men. The wings flaps and the landing gear were controlled by compressed air stored in tanks beneath the pilot's seat. It was towed by a C-47, the work horse of the English Air Force.

Just before take-off the wing commander had been disqualified. He had passed out, sick with strain. This added to the nerves of the men in that group.

The trip across the channel was reassuring. They saw many ships but no aircraft. They were cut loose from their tow planes over Normandy in the dark. The signal for landing was to be green flares. They saw the flares; then the message came that the flares and the landing area had been taken over by the Germans. They were told to turn left, toward Caen. Orders were confused. In maneuvering Vinton had to use his air and found that he could not control his flaps. Red balls flew around them from Cherbourg, shots from German Artillery. The Horsa was struck.

For Vinton there was total blackness and a loud drumming noise. He became conscious that he was on the ground and under the glider. He says,

"The Horsa was on my neck."

It was crumpled among the long poles, like telephone poles, set up by the enemy to entrap aircraft.

In time aid came to pull off the craft and get him out. But Vinton knew that his back was injured, his legs were paralyzed. He ordered the men to leave him until a medical man came to move him.

By the light of occasional flares he made out that there

was a deep ditch nearby. Wriggling on his stomach he managed to reach it and let himself down. There he lay all night while shells passed over. He was generally scratched up but that pain seemed minor. When he tried to move his legs, pain was intense. They would not function. Daylight hours — there was still shelling nearby. He took a book from his pocket and read. The detective story had seemed exciting before; now it was dull, but he turned pages.

He thought of Lois. She, too, had been waiting for June. Would it be a boy? Would he see him?

That afternoon he was found and loaded onto a jeep. But the driver had not traveled far when he was ordered to stop. The road ahead was covered by snipers. The driver, a slender boy, stood by the jeep. He would not take shelter because his passenger could not. They waited. Another pilot who knew Vinton came along, a Choctaw Indian. He asked Vinton what he was doing there. Vinton told him,

"Snipers up ahead."

The Choctaw said, "I'll take care of that."

He disappeared into the brushy woods along the road. He returned in about fifteen minutes. "No snipers," he said. "Go ahead."

When Vinton was unloaded onto the beach a doctor came to check his condition. Vinton told him, "I can wait." The doctor put a tag on him and went on to others.

Enemy planes were flying over. A jeep driver climbed onto a half truck which was equipped with an anti-air gun and fired at the planes. Vinton was admiring his presence of mind until he realized that his shots were going right across a gas tank-truck which was parked right next to him.

Finally on a LST (landing ship tank) with sides eight feet high, he felt comparatively secure. But he missed something — there was no view.

Back in England he was put in a hospital at Oxford. Because he was an officer he was given a private room. He would have preferred being in a ward with enlisted men, to hear them laugh and groan, curse and tell their stories. But his room was quiet. And then on the eighth of June, alone in the quiet room, he heard a baby cry.

He noted the time and he wrote to Lois. In a hospital in San Bernardino their son Michael had been born.

While Vinton was in the hospital, working hopefully to recover from paralysis, he learned that overall the action of the gliders on D Day had been a success. Much had been learned, in this primal venture, experience put to use in Southern France, against Germany, and in the Battle of the Bulge.

His back recovered and in a few days he began to walk again, haltingly, painfully, but he could walk. There were more months in the hospital and in France. In April, 1945, he returned to his home in the desert.

April is the month of flowers. The sands of the homestead were golden with dandelions and marigolds. And Lois — she was beautiful.

Michael had wide blue eyes and red-gold hair. He was learning to walk. Vinton watched him. How wonderful to walk!

Lois and Vinton have a home near the dry lake. Glider pilots and airmen often come to see them. There is a close bond between fliers and between the wives who shared the months of waiting. Many of them learned to love the desert and remember with pleasure the months at Condor Field.

Doctor from Harvard and Guadalcanal

Among the men returning from service was Doctor Edward Lincoln Smith. None could have been more welcome in our town. Doctor Smith was a commander in the U.S. Navy Medical Corps. He had been trained in the Harvard Medical School and had interned at the Rhode Island Hospital.

Nine months before Pearl Harbor he had enlisted, because he expected that war would come. He left a residency in obstetrics and was assigned to the Marine Corps. He remembers the sudden shift from New England's ivy halls to Quantico as "a bit of a shock."

By transport and by landing barge he had, in September of 1942, disembarked on the beach of Guadalcanal.

This once beautiful white beach, with its tall palms and bright birds was a scene of horror. The palms were frayed stumps and the sands were littered with the charred remains of Zeros, Japanese planes, which had burned with their pilots in them. The fresh battalion was greeted by gaunt, hungry-looking Marines who were exhausted and short of ammunition — too exhausted to show any emotion. They had survived the first landing and had been hanging on through bitter fighting for more than a month.

The new Marine battalion was ordered to unload and move their ammunition and supplies to the shelter of a grove well back of the beach. And they were ordered to dig themselves foxholes.

Before midnight they were awakened by flares dropped from planes, and immediately they were shelled from ships anchored offshore. Colonel Puller, the commander, could be heard telling his men to remain quiet and in the earth. When the attack ended Doctor Smith crawled from his fox-

Commander Edward Lincoln Smith. "No one could have been more welcome in our town."

Below: Vinton Harz meets his son Michael.

Photo, Twentynine Palms Library

hole to seek out the men who cried out in their agony. Near to his own shelter lay the body of a man, stripped of clothing, disemboweled, lying in a pool of blood. The doctor rolled the body in a poncho and went on to the next.

He worked through days of desperate fighting, nights when the Japanese war cry "Marine you die" rang out as the enemy gathered, bayonets in hand, for new attacks.

In the book "Marine" by Burke Davis, a man who was there tells of Doctor Smith operating on a crude table under a tarp which had been stretched across a gully. The ground on which he stood was a muck of blood and mud. One of his shoes had been sucked off, a foot was bare. He had been operating all night.

Colonel Puller, watching for a moment, said only, "Well, Doc, when they trained you at Harvard you never thought you'd come to this."

When the war ended and he had been discharged, Commander Smith, on his way home, planned to spend a few days in California. He thought it a pleasant place to which he might wish to return someday. He visited the Redlands Clinic, and there he was told that a town, Twentynine Palms, about one hundred miles distant in the Mojave Desert, had no doctor. Colonel Lee Watson, who had homesteaded there, was a patient in the Redlands hospital, and Doctor Smith went to his room and talked to him.

In earlier years there had been doctors in the community from time to time, and there had been nurses who were generous and concerned to give such help as they could, but during the war years there had been no doctor. Lee Watson advised him to go out and see the place for himself. Had he ever lived in a desert?

Doctor Smith is a man who lives to respond to need. Here there was need, and quiet, and welcome. He came and established an office in the Plaza. On the morning that he drove into town, his car full of luggage, he found a man waiting for him on the doorstep of his motel room. Taking his bag from the car he opened his door and gave the patient such treatment as he could to relieve his emphysema.

He would go on call, sometimes driving miles, day and night. He delivered babies in trailers and in remote homestead cabins where there was no running water or electricity. One day near Dead Man's Lake, while he was waiting for a mother's labor to progress, he was entertained by a child who proudly showed him a sidewinder asleep in a tree. In another cabin chickens wandered into the room while the baby was being born.

Often during the bloody fighting on Guadalcanal he had hoped that he might someday serve where his work was not to ease life out, but to welcome it.

Doctor Smith's mother, Martha Ann Smith, left her comfortable home in Vermont and came to join him and to assist in his office. We wondered that a woman who had lived always in New England could adapt to living in a desert area which, by her standards, was still crude. She loved it.

Not long after her arrival the doctor delivered a baby in a small house already crowded with children. The summer heat was stifling; the mother was exhausted, the baby fragile. Doctor Ed sent word to Martha Ann: "Prepare a room; I am bringing them home. The baby could not survive in the oven of this house."

Martha Ann was ready when they came. For two weeks she kept mother and child in her home until the baby was established in life and able to endure. Every evening the father would bring the other children to the house and they would all have ice cream together.

It was Martha Ann who told me this story. Two little girls, Barbara Dunn and my grandchild Linda, came to the door of the doctor's office, their eyes streaming tears. Barbara carried her doll; the head had been broken and was barely held together by the wig. There was no one waiting that morning. Doctor Ed took the girls to his inner office and put the doll on the examining table. With skilled fingers he restored the broken head and made it beautiful again. He sent the little girls away, their faces still tear streaked but smiling with happiness.

He was so much our friend. We accepted and did not often marvel that a man so trained would work under the primitive conditions of the desert; that a doctor who had operated for hours, standing barefoot in mud and blood, would delicately mend a doll.

Something More

These were happy years for Frank and me. Our sons returned. Alan and Denny went back to their universities. Both graduated with degrees in engineering. John, who was married and had a little girl, born while he was overseas, took over Frank's work as Wholesale Distributor for the Standard Oil Company.

This made it possible for Frank to take a vacation. We drove to the states where we had lived as children. In Oregon the dogwood was in bloom and in the dark woods I found the blossoms of wild currant, wet with dew and shining like rubies among the green.

Frank had longed to see the wheat fields of Washington. His father had been the first to grow wheat on the rolling hills (after he had been advised that it could not be done). The wheat was golden and rippling in the wind. He showed me the road where he had walked to school with a group of children. There had been a little girl; he never spoke to her although he had once carried her books. But in our college days, he had confided to me that he had loved her so deeply that he did not think it possible that he could ever love again.

In Spokane he rediscovered the trestle where he had once hung underneath while a train passed over — just to see how it would feel. There was another trestle he used to cross, leading his little sister, when they went to visit their mother's grave in a cemetery among the trees.

It was a wonderful trip, but when we returned to our home in the desert even the big mountain with the Indian head, bare and black at noon, looked beautiful to us.

Frank had his health, we were not in debt, we had the

fun of seeing our sons, our business, and our town grow up. Perhaps we had grown too. Frank said,

"What more can be asked of a country store?"

But I wanted something more.

Frank was no longer postmaster, and the office had been moved to a large building across the street. There was a vacant room. I used it to open a shop. There were in the town, in 1949, a drug store, a gift shop with novelties, clothing shops and a variety store. Absurdly, I attempted to carry everything else in household lines.

I had one principle. Things should be either useful or beautiful. When possible, they should be both. And I wanted to make it a place where local artists could display their pictures. Frank protested:

"You can't possibly sell can openers and expect an artist to want to hang his pictures in your shop."

But they did — and eventually we sold more paintings than can openers.

Irene Zimmers Charlton was the first to display her interpretations of the mysterious shadowed hills of the desert Sara Schenck brought in water colors. When I told her that Art Krushat's wife wanted to buy her picture of the Oasis of Mara, she exclaimed, "Oh, I'll give it to her."

We sold on commission and for a time it was difficult to separate business from the informal and friendly ways of the town.

John Hilton, a professional artist, nationally acclaimed, had brought a landscape. A visitor to Twentynine Palms was considering it. But the wife of the plumber came, saw the painting, and said:

"I'll take that. It is beautiful. John Hilton wants my husband to put in a septic tank for him. They can work out a deal."

Later in the day the tourist came in to buy. He said it had been the only picture he ever wanted.

I called the place "Helen Bagley's Shop" so the market manager wouldn't try to take it over. In time it was recognized by artists and public.

One morning a woman, a gentle grey ghost, who took long walks through the village to assuage her loneliness, entered the door. She said,

"I came out looking for beauty, and I have already found it, in your window." This was a rewarding moment.

Our shop remained a place where people were welcome to come "just looking."

John lived near and grandchildren dropped in. I remember Kathy, her face smeared by a chocolate ice cream cone, conducting her friends around "Grandma's store" and discussing the pictures displayed. She has remained a student of art.

"Little John," age four, the cowboy stage of growing up, always carried a rifle. This was a hazard to china and glass arranged on open shelves. I put a hook on a peg board near the entrance and reminded him that cowboys always stacked their weapons when entering a room. He never forgot to hang his weapon on its special hook.

The women who worked with me understood children. We made them welcome; they caused us anxious moments but never any loss.

Bessie Louise Flickinger, a lovely and serene woman from the South, was the mother of five grown children. She enjoyed working with beautiful things, but it bothered her to think of the shop as a business with a profit motive — however dim. I once watched her wrap a Pyrex mixing bowl as a wedding gift. She put it in a large white box, packed it with fine shredded paper, wrapped it in gift paper and tied it with a large ribbon bow on top. The materials were more costly than the bowl.

"There," she said happily, "It does my heart good to do something like this."

Carmen Boyer did much to bring about our success with art. She was a slight, bright woman with a surprising range of abilities. Her husband was an artist, highly original and talented. And that is a story worth telling.

She had brought him to the desert because of an incurable lung condition resembling silicosis. Their doctor in San Francisco had advised her,

"He may live five months or five years. He will feel better in dry air."

He was a proud man. His father had owned a plantation in Cuba and there was much of the Latin tradition of machismo in Merritt Boyer. His career had been in the army where he was an officer, and in teaching. He had never allowed his wife to work.

He would not consent to her coming to Twentynine Palms to arrange a place to live; he must drive with her and decide everything. When they arrived at a motel, worn out with the long trip in a small car, the motel manager refused them a room. She thought Merritt was about to die of tuberculosis.

They found a cabin where plaster dropped from the wall. During the first year, Carmen with her own hands, built a house. Her husband, too ill to help with the labor, told her just how to build. Painting it was a luxury, but he could assist with that.

Their savings had been used and it was necessary that she work. She worked in the office of our market and later as manager in the shop. This left Merritt alone with the frustration of idleness and the misery of dependence.

Then Carmen found that he had taken the odd bits of house paint and made pictures on any bare space he could find, including the inside of the privy door. And they were good.

Extravagantly she bought oil paint, brushes and canvas. His father had been an artist, a Sunday painter. Merritt had never painted before and he had no opportunity to study, but he did not paint as a primitive.

He was a mathematician and an intellectual. These qualities entered his art. He designed angular puppet figures, so clear and concise that the body lines, with no faces drawn, expressed loneliness, yearning, and sometimes the joyous sense of freedom in the arid wideness of the desert. In many of his pictures there is a subtle humor, as distinctive

An autograph party for John Hilton when SONORA SKETCHBOOK was republished. Left to right: Mrs. James Cagney, John Hilton, Helen Bagley, June Feldman, Barbara Hilton.

Painting by Merritt Boyer, LEAPYEAR COURTSHIP. "Angular puppet figures, the body lines expressed loneliness, yearning — a subtle humor, as distinctive as a signature."

as a signature. His first show was in our shop. When I entered the room that morning I was amazed at the beauty of line and fresh color. A few collectors bought at once.

Then Carmen did a brave and a very unsophisticated thing. She packed a suitcase with his pictures and in her vacation time she took this into Hollywood. With a friend to help carry the suitcase she tramped the hot streets of the art section of the city. Some galleries would not deign to look, some admired but turned her away. One gallery accepted and arranged a one-man show.

This gave Merritt confidence. He had been sure of his work but uncertain of recognition. He began to prepare for a show in New York City.

A famous artist, visiting the local gallery, chanced to see a painting of Merritt's stored in a closet. He inquired and came to find Carmen. Taking her aside, into our cluttered wrapping room, he told her,

"Your husband is a genius."

When Carmen told me about it, afterwards, she cried. I had never seen her shed tears before.

Aware that he was slowly dying, depending more and more on pure oxygen for breath, Merritt once spoke to me from the plastic folds of an oxygen tent. He said,

"When you know that there is not much time left, then every little thing becomes exquisite."

And this perception he expressed as long as he could hold a brush.

The Twentynine Palms Artist's Guild was organized in 1951 with seven professional members. Their meeting was held in the Boyer home, because Merritt was too disabled to leave it.

It was the same year that the Marine Corps came to this desert. They took over the Base and a large territory surrounding it, dry lakes and mountains. Some people were fearful that the character of the town would be changed. But Frank and I came to know the Marines through community affairs, as well as in the Shop. Many a Marine has told us that they felt themselves welcomed here. They entered into the life of the town, contributing youth and mature experience. They widened our horizons beyond the mountains and the valleys to oceans and lands around the world.

Marine wives admit that they have a saying, "You cry when you come and you cry when you leave." More than a few Marines, after retiring, returned to make their homes.

Gradually we added books to our stock, books about the desert, children's books, and a small general selection. The Marines had their own library. When one lost a book he had checked out he was required to bring the Shop an order to replace it. The range of their interests, especially in technical books, was revealing. One day a young corporal, the pink of his cheeks still showing beneath the tan of training camp, brought in a slip. He had lost a book entitled, "Life and Love for Teenagers." It was entirely appropriate, just surprising.

I remember, too, an older man who wanted to order twenty titles of Zane Grey. I got down the catalogue and copied carefully. He apologized for the trouble he was causing.

"It is all I can manage to read," he said. "My son has been killed. I have no one else."

I, too, had known sorrow and we talked awhile.

My Shop was never so busy or successful that there was not time for people. It could keep the spirit of the old store.

When we could give a show for an artist or an autographing party for an author — that was an occasion. It compensated for many hours of dusting and hopefully rearranging Pyrex and can openers. One author, Adelaide Arnold, for whom we planned a party, declined at the last moment to go through with it. She was too shy. Another, the author of "The Late Liz" was not shy at all, but she regretfully told us that her publisher said she must never admit to anybody that she had written the book. She later sold several thousand in paperback. No one sued her and the sky did not fall.

When we had a party for John Hilton, celebrating a new

edition of "Sonora Sketch Book," he also brought us paintings. This, for our small business, was a triumph.

Betty Campbell wrote her book "The Desert Was Home" and came for a party. Her husband Bill had been killed in an accident twelve years before. She had sold her mansion built of native stone, feeling her loss so overwhelming that she could not live there alone. She had lived in Nevada and in Arizona.

She had become increasingly deaf and it was hard for her to meet people. At her request I arranged for Frank to sit beside her and repeat for her the greetings of her friends.

Frank and I had known, more perhaps than anyone else, of the community work and gifts that the Campbells had contributed to Twentynine Palms. But now people told us of kindness and care, personal and quiet, sometimes in remote areas of the desert; deeds unknown to any others.

Betty felt herself warmly welcomed. She sold her house in Tucson and came home. She built another colonial house upon a hill. In the yard she made a laboratory in which she stored and classified a large part of the Indian artifacts, collected in this area. These she gave to the National Park Service for the museum in the headquarters of the Joshua Tree National Monument, near the Oasis of Mara.

When we had been 29 years in Twentynine Palms there was a town party for us. It was a delightful and heartwarming affair, not only for us, but because it brought together old friends, homesteaders, who had not seen each other for decades.

"Bagley Day" had been planned by a group of our friends. Letters had been sent to people who had moved from the community, inviting them to the party and asking for letters and snapshots to be assembled in an album, and for telegrams to be read.

Tables had been set on the lawn of the Twentynine Palms Inn, tables with white cloths and flowers. People brought their own food. A program had been arranged. Sherman Clark had been chairman of the committee for the program. Sherm was growing blind, but as the darkness closed his spiritual vision grew more clear. Aided always by the graciousness and tact of his wife Amo, he devoted his talent for leadership to many causes of benefit to the community. Now even to this party, a celebration of friendship and of the adventures of the early settlers.

He could not share the scene of the white clothed tables grouped on the lawn below the palm trees; nor could he recognize the faces of those who came to greet him. But he always said, "I'm glad to see you." And his response made the day seem brighter.

Robert McCown, "Bob," who helped us set up our first gas pump was master of ceremonies, presiding with charm and humor. There was an orchestra, and Allie Wrubel had composed two songs, "Twentynine Years in Twentynine Palms" and the "Bagley Calypso" for which castanets accompained the words of the chorus, "Rattlesnakes a'rattling in Rattlesnake canyon."

Doctor Luckie had honored us by coming from Pasadena, and Veda and Ben Benioff, long happily married, had driven out. Of course, our sons and grandchildren were there.

A skit was staged. Bill Smith, dressed once more in his bib overalls, had a part, Lida Donnell, as charming as ever, and Art and Heinie from the store.

The skit ran thus:

"What no matches! I've driven thirty miles and you don't have any matches? What the hell kind of a store is this?"

"I'd drive all the way to Banning to get a loaf of bread rather than pay you two cents more for it."

"Frank, I see you have some nice new canvas water bags. Would you loan me one for a few days until I can get into Sears to buy one?"

"Just charge the oil. Charge it to McCown. He owes me some money and he said this would be OK."

We laughed with the crowd, remembering. But we remembered also the tolerance and kindness of the home-

steaders for two people who thought that just anyone could
run a grocery store.

Frank and I were amazed that friends with important
affairs would have taken time for such an occasion. We felt
as though we had been at our own funeral, but this was
much more fun — and we have had time to remember.

When Frank was called to speak in response to tributes
he said, "What Twentynine Palms had done for the Bagleys
is much more than anything the Bagleys have done for
Twentynine Palms."

Then it was my turn to respond. I told of Ivy Hockett
who had helped us adjust to desert living. She had confided
to me,

"You spoiled things when you came."

She had not meant to be unkind, and she explained.
"Before you opened your store we homesteaders would get
together when supplies were about to run out. Each would
bring what he had and we would have a dinner. The next
day we would all go to town and stock up."

I would have liked that too. And now when sometimes I
find myself nostalgic for the days of frontier life, tempted
to be resentful of the modern and progressive, I remember
that we "spoiled things when we came."

Even that was many years ago.

When we had kept store for forty years we sold to
younger men. Art and Heinie had already retired. We continued the Shop for a few more years, and we have missed
the interesting contacts it brought us.

Now there are all the businesses and organizations, useful and necessary for a town. A few I wish to name because
they seem to me to be unique, or just because they are so
welcome:

The hospital, built by Dr. William Ince as a memorial to
his father, Thomas H. Ince. It saved many lives.

The Recreation District, which took over the swimming
pool built by the Legion years before, enlarged it and made
a grassy park for games on summer evenings — Luckie
Park.

Doctor James Luckie and Frank Bagley at "29 Years in 29 Palms" party, Bagley Day, 1957.

Prescription blank reads: "The thought came to me when I first saw the valley: If scenes like these thy heart can share Then bide a welcome pilgrim here."

The palm trees planted along the principal streets by the Lion's Club.

The Artists' Guild and the Artist's Work Shop, for the artists, have increased our awareness of form and color in the desert landscape.

I marvel at the vision of the men who, when Twentynine Palms was hardly a village, planned the Civic Center, so that now there is the County Building and the Library across Adobe Road from the "Little Church of the Desert."

And I am grateful to the men and women of The Twentynine Palms Corporation who gave the land of the Oasis of Mara to the Joshua Tree National Monument. The primeval beauty is protected and today one may walk beneath the towering palms.

Good things like these are in many towns. But because we have seen this one grow from a few scattered homesteads, we can realize how they come to be. The men who work for the community now have the spirit of the pioneers who with their hands — and backs — built the first schoolhouse, and the roads.

The delight in wilderness, the adventure of the frontier — these have passed. But there remain kindness and concern, and the challenge to initiative and courage in a changing world.

And there are wide spaces and the stars.

A Town

Man does not live by bread alone
A city is not built of stone.
God is revealed in human kind
In magnanimity and mind
In will to labor and to give
In love which makes the spirit live.
A town is made from gifts like these.
Time adds the grace of arching trees.